GOD'S
GLOVES

D1323161

Other titles by Jennifer Rees-Larcombe:

Beyond Healing (Hodder and Stoughton 1986)

Books for Children:
Auntie Maude's Windmill
The Fire Brand
The Broken Stone
Dance to the Music
(Marshall Pickering)

GOD'S
GLOVES

Giving and receiving care

JENNIFER
REES-LARCOMBE

Marshall Pickering

Bible references are taken from the Good News Bible, The New International Version, The Authorised Version and The Living Bible

Marshall Morgan and Scott
Marshall Pickering
3 Beggarwood Lane, Basingstoke,
Hants RG23 7LP, UK

British Library Cataloguing in Publication Data

Rees-Larcombe, Jennifer
    God's gloves: giving and receiving care.
    1. Christian life—1960-
    I. Title
    248.4   BV4501.2

    ISBN 0–551–01423–7

Text Phototypeset in Linotron Plantin by
Input Typesetting Ltd, London SW19 8DR
Printed in Great Britain by Anchor Brendon Ltd,
Tiptree, Essex.

To all the anonymous people who have allowed me to use their experiences in this book.

And to Grace and Mary who have prayed for it daily.

Contents

Preface		9
Foreword		12
1:	No arms to cuddle sad people	15
2:	The lady on the pedestal	23
3:	I'm shy	29
4:	What if I don't feel loving?	34
5:	I'm frightened of becoming too involved	42
6:	What if I become a doormat?	47
7:	I don't have enough to share	54
8:	I haven't the time	63
9:	I never seem to be successful	72
10:	Danger! Families at risk	77
11:	I'm too ill to be useful to God	92
12:	I'm on my own	96
13:	I feel too depressed myself	100
14:	I have no gifts	104
15:	What are our motives for serving God?	107
16:	How does our church look from the outside?	119
17:	Taking the roof off our church	126
18:	Love your neighbour	140
19:	God's gloves at work	150
20:	I was sick and you visited me	157
21:	Bereavement	160
22:	Helping in a crisis	170
23:	Caring for the carers	175
24:	Loving by post	178
25:	The non-professionals	183

Preface

Probably most of the people who open this book will not really have time to read it at all! Their lives may be crammed to bursting point with all kind of activities; an absorbing career with church work in their spare time, elderly parents to care for, or a home and family to run. I haven't tried to write a deep theological tome (actually I couldn't if I tried!) This is a practical book about a practical way of serving God, and I have tried to break it down into short sections that could be read while waiting for the eggs to boil, or your hair to dry or while travelling on the underground to work.

It may seem rather strange to find a disabled woman writing a book about showing love in active ways, but five years ago when I was first asked to write it, I was fit, healthy and full of energy, and in my enthusiasm I had soon filled a large notebook. Seven years before that, on a cold January day God had done something very extraordinary for me which blasted me right out of my insular, houseproud, family-absorbed life, and opened my eyes to the needs of the people around me. Looking back, I can see that God turned me inside out, and cured my shyness and my many feelings of inadequacy. Those years stand out as the happiest in my life so far, but I cringe when I remember some of the mistakes I made as I first tried to act as 'God's gloves'. Then suddenly I became disabled with a disease rather like Multiple Sclerosis, and was no longer able to do much for other people, let alone myself and six children. Sadly, I put away the bulging notebook and forgot about it. There it lay under my winter jumpers at the back of the drawer until I realised I had learnt far more about the art of caring by being cared for, than ever I had by caring for others myself! So I dug out the notebook and viewed what I had written from the far side of the fence.

I knew if I wrote this book it would have to be a patchwork made up of the experiences of many people, and not just my own. So I began writing letters on my specially adapted electric typewriter asking my friends for help. It was then that I ran into trouble. They were all most reluctant to talk about their work for God. Jesus told us to keep our acts of practical love so secret that our left hand won't know what our right hand is doing! He promises a reward only to those who obey Him in this silence. Therefore, they felt that by talking to me they were betraying that trust. I had to persuade them that they might be helping people just be telling their stories of God in action. That is why I have had to change their names and disguise things here and there.

These people are not 'superstars', just ordinary people like us, often feeling just as inadequate as we do. Sometimes the story they told me was the only time God used them in that way. Don't read this book and feel that you have to help people in all the different kinds of situations I mention. God just wants us to be available to Him to use if and when He needs us. He does the work, we are just His gloves.

The word 'caring' has become part of our Christian jargon and I will try to use it as little as possible. However, in the context of this book, when I mention caring I mean minding deeply about how other people are feeling, and trying under God's control to do something practical to help. As John says in his first letter, chapter 3:18 (GNB), 'Our love should not be just words and talk, it must be pure love which shows itself in action'.

10

By reading through a book like this there is no possibility that any of us will become experts on helping people in need, nor will a lifetime of experience equip us either! Every person we meet will be different and will require a unique kind of help and support. I have been told some tragic stories of the way suffering people have been hurt even more by the well-meaning, but misguided attempts of Christians to help them. The greatest lesson I have learnt through writing this book, is the vital necessity of allowing God to show us on every occasion what He wants us to do, when He wants us to do it, and how it is to be done!

Foreword

It was mid-morning and the house was buzzing with a happy babble of noise. Three pre-schoolers were crashing around on the kitchen table with lumps of dough, supposedly creating something edible.

In the lounge, a young woman, her leg heavily bandaged, was reclining on the settee. She and her motorbike had parted company at the bottom of the drive earlier that day.

It was on this occasion that I first met Jen. She had welcomed me, together with a friend, into her home for a cup of coffee and other refreshments. Immediately, her whole being drew me to Jesus. I was quite overcome by the sense of love, graciousness and welcoming that seem to pour out of her. Nothing was too much for Jen. Individual needs were met without preferential treatment being given to anyone.

Having known Jen over the years and heard much about her from others, I know there is no one better qualified to write such a book as *God's Gloves*. She writes from the perspective of a giver, though now, because of her disabilities, she has to be on the receiving end of much love and concern from her family.

Jen draws on many anecdotes and situations from the past, as well as the experiences of people close to her. She presents a comprehensive account of what it means to work out Christian faith in social action. The book is fast-moving, and often amusing, challenging us to get on with the job and leave the results in God's hands.

The world today is in crisis. The Church has sadly

neglected its responsibilities during the last century. Rather than demonstrating to others our love and commitment to Jesus Christ, we have allowed those with different persuasions and religions beliefs to step into the gap. We have become a pale shadow of Christians before us, who fought hard for changes in society; prison and hospital reform, working hours and conditions, trade unions and child care, abolition of slavery.

I recommend that we take *God's Gloves*, and through the empowering of the Holy Spirit, allow the challenge it offers to be worked out in our lives. As we read it, let the words of James 2:15-17 (NIV), echo in our hearts.

'Suppose a brother or sister is without clothers and daily food. If one of you says to him, "Go, I wish you well; keep warm and well fed," but does nothing about his physical needs, what good is it? In the same way, faith by itself, if it is not accompanied by action, is dead.'

Ruth Calver
September 1986

1: No arms to cuddle sad people

One cold January day, twelve years ago, I remember vividly going to meet my five year old son from school. I knew something was wrong as he trailed across the playground to meet me. His thick grey socks drooped dismally down his matchstick legs, and his lunch bag bumped along the ground behind him like a miserable puppy dog. Framed by the hood of his grey dufflecoat his little white, tear stained face looked pathetically up at me.

'What went wrong?' I asked anxiously.

'*Everything,*' was the tragic reply. 'The teacher was cross, my sums wouldn't come right and nobody cared about me all day long.'

'Never mind,' I said hugging him, 'today is the day we are going into town to buy those new shoes with laces; and,' I added recklessly, 'we'll pop into a café first and have a doughnut.'

By this time his big sister Sarah had joined us, (maddeningly pleased with the star she had got for her table test) and we all piled into the car together.

As we drove through the new housing estate where we lived then, and over the common to fight for a parking place near the shops, not even the thought of the doughnut could lift Justyn's spirits and restore him to his usual happy self. He really must have had a very bad day indeed. Sarah did her best to be bracing.

'You couldn't feel lonely in the playground because I'm there, and you know the dinner ladies never let people bully the little ones.'

'But you can feel lonely inside,' retorted Justyn.

'Well you shouldn't,' continued Sarah piously, 'Jesus is always with you, even in the toilet.'

'Yes, but,' put in the aggrieved Justyn, 'Jesus hasn't got arms any more to cuddle sad people.'

This childish remark was so true that it hit me like a physical blow as I swung into the multi-storey car park.

As we walked along the crowded pavements of the busy shopping centre, I looked into the faces of the other shoppers – looked at them as I never had before. I noticed lines of strain and worry etched deeply on them, and pain behind their eyes. Most of them looked as if 'no-one had cared for them all day' either. Loneliness and misery cannot be hidden behind layers of make-up.

I deemed it wiser to get the doughnut safely into Justyn and thus avoid a hunger tantrum in the shoe shop. But as we hurried towards the café, we were nearly run over by a pram pushed by a harassed young mother. She was very overweight and her hair and clothes were a mess. She looked desolate – gone to seed. Two babies were squashed into the pram and a bawling toddler clutched her dirty coat.

'Dad,dad,da,' remarked the smaller of the two babies and I wondered if Dad was one of the many unemployed, or had he walked out on them altogether? As I looked at the hopeless expression on that girl's face, I rather thought he had, and I felt uncomfortable inside.

Our favourite café was far too crowded for us to get seats, so we had to go round the corner to the 'Singing Kettle' – a much more genteel establishment. They were crowded too, but there were just three seats left at a table already occupied by an elderly lady – a real 'Tunbridge Wells type' – and she looked thoroughly horrified when we squeezed in beside her. As we ordered our doughnuts, coke and a pot of tea for me, I glanced across the table at her from this new strange angle. I noticed the expensive coat and hat, and the leather gloves that clutched the matching bag. But the corners of her mouth turned down in an expression of endless hopelessness, and I couldn't help wondering if she was not worse off than the young mum we had just encountered, who at least had three human beings who needed her, while this lady looked as if no-one had cared for her in years. There are thousands like her in Tunbridge Wells.

I shook myself and sipped my China tea. Why was I suddenly getting depressed like this? We had our lovely shiny modern house on the estate – these two lovely children, and little Naomi whom I had left with my mother so we could buy the shoes in peace. Tony had a steady job, we were happy in our church, and had been Christians for years. What was the matter with me? All my time was taken up with being a good housewife and mother, surely God wanted me to do just that – but for good measure I was a Sunday school teacher as well, and helped run a monthly Outreach coffee morning.

Fortified by the refreshments, we walked out into the wind and sleet. It was nearly five o'clock now and women were dashing home from work, tired and strained but still with a meal to get, housework to do and perhaps a pile of ironing. Everyone was pushing and shoving their way along the pavement – just existing. No-one smiled. They were locked into their own narrow lives. What was wrong with me? 'Hurry up,' I told myself firmly, 'buy the shoes and get back to your own safe little world.'

The shoes were hideously expensive, and I was more depressed than ever as we sat in the traffic jam waiting to get out of the car park. I remembered those empty strained faces, and thought about a radio report I had heard while washing up that morning. 'Depression among women,' it said, 'has so increased over the last five years that it has reached epidemic proportions. Tranquillizers are now the most prescribed of any drug, and not only is alcoholism increasingly rapidly among young people, but it is also called the disease of the middle-aged housewife'.

A town like Tunbridge Wells looks so nice on the outside. Tourists come to see it in the summer and stay in the expensive hotels, but under the surface there is pain, fear and misery. 'So what are you doing about it Lord?' I asked as we moved at last out into the crowded street. Then I definitely felt Him reply, 'What are *you* doing about it? I have no arms nowadays to cuddle sad people.'

'But Lord,' I said, 'what can I do? I'm up to my eyes with three kids and keeping the house nice.' The children were playing 'I spy' in the back, and the sleet was making life hard for my windscreen wipers, but suddenly I felt I *saw* Jesus. I remember the very place on the road where it happened, and I can never drive past there without remembering it. His face was twisted with grief, as He watched all those hopeless, miserable people. He could help them, but He needed my arms, my smile, my love to do it for Him.

It was a terrible rush getting the meal done, putting Naomi into her cot, and settling the others off to bed. I always get terribly flustered when I've got a baby-sitter coming, and feel I must spring clean the whole house for her. This was no ordinary evening. This was the evening we were going to join the house group down the road. Our church was so big that the vicar had formed small groups combining discussion and Bible study for people who lived near to one another. Ours had been going quite a long time, but we had not been all that keen to join in. I always felt exhausted after chasing Naomi all day, and Tony hated turning out once he was home in the evening. But we really had felt we ought to put in an appearance now and then, and tonight was our first night.

The sleet had stopped when we peeped cautiously out

of our front door and the stars were appearing, even the moon slipped out from behind a cloud.

'We'll walk,' said Tony. 'It's only to the other side of the estate after all.'

'I'm taking my umbrella,' I said doubtfully as we set off.

All the houses on our estate looked oddly the same. Of course, some were detached, others were semis and there were a few very nice terraces, but they were all built by the same firm and they all looked alike. Each one stood behind its neat little front garden, and the tightly closed curtains revealed nothing of what went on inside.

'How cosy they all look,' remarked Tony happily. But I had heard enough gossip at the school gate to know that often the lives behind the curtains were far from happy. Not, of course, that I had time to get involved. We all lived very self-contained lives, busy with our own affairs. All the same, I knew that in number seven they had a spastic child who was so much like a vegetable they never took her out. Next door, the teenage daughter had anorexia and weighed only five stone. Pity, she'd been doing so well at school. I wondered how her mother felt shut up in the house with her all day. She had to stay in, I'd heard, because the kid kept threatening suicide. Then, of course, there was the doctor who lived next to us. His wife was slowly dying from cancer. I hadn't liked to call. I had never met her when she was well, and it looked nosy barging in now. She hardly had any visitors from what I could see from my spotlessly clean windows.

Everyone in the road knew about the Ransans. He was a civil servant and his wife was a huge woman. She must have weighed twenty stone at least. Some nights he would knock her about, and she would run screaming down the road. Tony and I treated it as a huge joke, but was it really so funny for her?

At number twelve, Robin had just walked out leaving no address or note, only a frantic wife and two tiny children.

'You're awfully quiet tonight,' said Tony.

'I was just thinking they're not all as happy as they look,' I said thoughtfully.

We arrived at last at our destination. About twelve other people were already there, and they made us feel wonderfully welcome. They worshipped the Lord so enthusiastically in the singing and prayers. Afterwards the leader gave an excellent and very well prepared Bible study. Then came the coffee and biscuits, and a girl I knew really well plonked herself down beside me. She was one of the leaders of the Outreach coffee morning.

'Alright for Thursday morning?' she asked brightly. 'We've got a really well known speaker coming this month and we do want a big crowd to show her what we can do, so don't forget to bring your fish.'

'Fish?' I said blankly. I thought I'd promised to bring biscuits.

'You know,' she laughed, 'an unconverted friend.' I had a terrible mental picture of all the Christian women converging on this girl's house followed by fish squirming on the end of tight leads. I knew I would not be welcome, or treated as one of the 'In' crowd unless I dug someone up from somewhere, but who could I take? I hadn't troubled since we moved in really to get to know people who did not go to our church. I was acquainted with plenty of them, but they could hardly be described as 'fish'.

'You look a little troubled this evening,' said the leader sitting down with his coffee on my other side. 'Did you not enjoy the meeting?'

'Oh yes,' I assured him. 'It was lovely, but I had this odd feeling today. Some of the people who live on the estate are in such misery – it suddenly worried me.'

He looked vaguely at me over his coffee cup.

'We don't tend to know any of our non-Christian neighbours,' he said. 'We're really too busy doing the Lord's work,' and he got up abruptly to join the 'In' crowd.

'What *was* doing the Lord's work?' I thought miserably as we walked home. That night my daily portion of the Bible seemed to leap out of the page and hit me in the eye.

When the son of Man comes in his glory, and all the angels with him, he will sit on his throne in heavenly glory. All the nations will be gathered before him and he will separate the people one from another as a shepherd separates the sheep from the goats. He will put the sheep on his right and the goats on his left.

Then the King will say to those on his right, 'Come, you who are blessed by my Father; take your inheritance, the kingdom prepared for you since the creation of the world. For I was hungry and you gave me something to eat, I was thirsty and you gave me something to drink, I was a stranger and you invited me in, I needed clothes and you clothed me, I was sick and you looked after me, I was in prison and you came to visit me.'

Then the righteous will answer him, 'Lord when did we see you hungry and feed you, or thirsty and give you something to drink? When did we see you a stranger and invite you in or needing clothes and clothed you? When did we see you sick or in prison and go to visit you?

The King will reply, 'I tell you the truth, whatever you did for one of the least of these brothers of mine you did for me' (Matt. 25:31 – 40 NIV).

I sat up in bed while the tears splashed down onto the pages of my Bible as I remembered the look of anguish I had seen on the face of Jesus earlier that day. He was not suffering in crucifixion – He had done that once and for all and was now risen into glory, but He was still suffering for the sad people who lived in my town, and my road, who needed His arms to cuddle them.

I saw again all the people pushing and shoving their way along the crowded pavement. This world lives for Number One. Does Christ not call us to be different? He laid down His life for His friends, and for a lost world, so as his disciple shouldn't I be doing the same thing?

'You know,' I said to Tony, and was answered by a crackle from his *Daily Telegraph*, 'Love is not just a gift or a fruit of the Spirit.' Another crackle from the paper. 'Love is a *command* with no by-passes. So how do we show love to people?'

The paper collapsed and he looked at me over its crumpled wall, but I answered my own question.

'I think it must be by doing practical things for people. Things God would do if He were here in person.'

2: The lady on the pedestal

Some days just seem to stick out like milestones in the memory. The day I have just described was like that for me. I wish I could say that it caused me to rush out and become a positive spiritual explosion in all the houses in my district. It did not. In fact, I think it only revealed to me my own personal inadequacies. If Jesus had been me living in my road, He would have known just what to do for all the sad and pressured people behind those curtains. I didn't know what I could do for any of them, and I had many personal 'hang-ups' which prevented me from even wanting to reach out of my cosy little nest towards them. I read and re-read the Gospels to see what Jesus actually did say and do. We can know the Bible from babyhood, and yet miss what it is really saying.

Jesus came to this earth to be punished by death as our substitute. To die in our place for our sin was the only way to make it possible for our souls to approach God and live with Him for ever. Of course, our souls are more important than our bodies which will soon be no good to us at all. But Jesus earned the right to talk to people about spiritual concepts by caring about their bodies, sharing their worries and sorrows, feeding the hungry and healing the sick. He even assisted Peter with his tax problems.

As I thought about the coffee morning to which I was supposed to drag along a fish on a line, I felt myself prickling all over with embarrassment. People weren't just fish to be caught, and then left to get on with it while we dashed off to dredge up another soul. God wanted me to befriend them for their own sakes just as Jesus loved and cared about *whole* people and not just souls. Then I would have earned the right to help them on a spiritual level. But as I hoovered and polished my house, I realised I did not really love my neighbours at all. Of course, it was quite different with my friends at church. We were so glad to meet on a Sunday morning, we would hug and kiss like real brothers and sisters. Ours was such a big church that you could only know a small proportion of the congregation, and I realised that we gravitated to people who we naturally liked, and with whom we had many things in common. Dimly I became aware that there was a fringe of people on the outside of all the happy little church cliques. People with emotional hang-ups and difficult personalities, and those who failed to fit into the stereotype slots. They stood around at the back of the church after the services, but no one bothered to talk to them.

Was our church just like a social club where we went to meet stimulating people? Jesus did not just love and care about the 'good' easy-to-like people. He befriended prostitutes, quislings, thieves and revolutionaries.

'Lord,' I prayed, 'I am very willing to serve you, but I have so many limitations. I don't mind doing specific jobs for you like Sunday school teaching, cleaning the church brasses or being on the flower rota – surely that's all you can expect of me at this busy stage in my life?' Even as I prayed, I realised that He commanded us all to love as He loved, a full time twenty-four hour a day job. If everyone in our church really loved like that, everyone in the parish and soon the whole town, would be reached for God, but we don't. Perhaps other people feel just as conscious of their limitations as I did. I have always found it far easier to think clearly if I write things down, and my Bible bulges with odd scraps of paper. I found the stub of a pencil in Justyn's drawing box and wrote down this list as I sat at my kitchen table.

I'm terribly shy.
I'm frightened of becoming just a doormat.
I'm not a naturally loving person.
I'm frightened of getting too involved or out of my depth.
I really haven't got the time.
Nothing I do ever seems to succeed.
My husband/wife would not like it. My children might suffer.
I feel too down myself – I've enough worries of my own.
I have no gifts that God could use.
I'm in need of help and support myself.
I'm on my own, I have to look after myself.
I have financial worries. I certainly have nothing to share.

The list was daunting. Most those items on the list were my problems, not just other people's. Thankfully, I realised it was time to go and meet the children from school and I pulled on my coat and woolly hat. There on the washing machine lay my gloves, limp and lifeless – no use to anyone; but as I put my hands inside them, suddenly they took on a new life.

'Don't worry about all your limitations,' God seemed to say. 'I'm not asking you to love people in your own strength. All I want is for you to be like those limp gloves. I have no human body now so let me put myself into you, just as you put your hands into these gloves. Then I can work for people through you. Even if you feel inadequate, I can still use you.'

It is twelve years since that milestone day, and since then I must have made every mistake possible. Yet God has led me into situations where I could watch Him removing my hang-ups and turning me inside out. While

25

at other times He has used me in spite of my limitations and sometimes because of them!

What follows is just a series of fragments gleaned over the years. Mistakes I have made, ideas I have tried, stories I have heard and things I have observed other people doing while they have tried both successfully and unsuccessfully to be God's gloves.

My first lesson

One morning soon after my 'milestone day', I woke feeling the ceiling must certainly have fallen on my head. As I groped my way to the bathroom looking for Disprin, I remembered with horror what day it was. I just could not have a headache that morning. Mrs. Stevens was coming to coffee.

A week previously, I had heard this 'spiritual super-star' speaking at a coffee morning on the subject of love. I had been so blessed, I had plucked up the courage to speak to her afterwards. Surely she would be able to counsel me about my desire to be God's gloves.

'I'll pop in and see you next week,' she had promised, 'then we'll have more time to talk.' I had felt so honoured I had nearly fainted. In those days I still minded about being a perfect housewife, and if someone was coming in for coffee I liked everything to look just right. But Mrs. Stevens wasn't just anybody. I wanted to put out for her, if not the red carpet, at least my best wedding present cups.

Everything was against me that morning. The children managed to reduce the house to chaos before I positively kicked them out to school, and as fast as I tidied up the mess after they had gone, little Naomi untidied it again. The washing machine decided to have a headache as well, and flooded the kitchen floor. Naomi's milk boiled all over the stove top, and as I took my best china from the cupboard one of the cups slipped and smashed on the puddly floor. Then to crown everything, my terrible old iron overheated yet again and singed a hole in Tony's nylon shirt.

By the time I heard the doorbell I was practically hysterical. Longing to make a good impression on this lady whom I had placed on such a high pedestal, I just had time to hide the two over-loaded baskets of ironing under the kitchen table and dash for the front door.

'How lovely to see you,' I gushed, but she was far too wise to be taken in.

'My dear, you look as if you have a headache,' she said gently. Suddenly I found myself telling her about the washing machine, milk and broken cup.

'Do you know what I am going to do?' she said firmly. 'I'm going to fill a hot water bottle, and see you into bed. I'll keep an eye on your little girl while you sleep this thing off.' I was horrified. If I was upstairs she would discover all my inefficiencies – she might even find my heaps of neglected ironing. I made a feeble protest, but she swept me up to bed before I really knew what was happening. It must have been about two hours later when I woke feeling wonderfully better. When I saw the time, I sprang out of bed and hurried downstairs feeling highly embarrassed. Something extraordinary had happened! It was as if a magic wand had been waved over the whole house. Everywhere was tidy, dusted and polished, even the house plants looked rejuvenated. Naomi was deeply absorbed in drawing pictures at the kitchen table and those menacing mountains of ironing now lay folded, immaculate and subdued in the airing cupboard.

'You look much better dear,' said Mrs. Stevens. 'I must dash, I have a meeting to speak at in half an hour.'

I had never had time to ask her about how to be more loving, but I did not need words from her. She had demonstrated to me all I needed to know.

That evening when I went to put out the empty milk bottles, I found a parcel on the doormat.

'This comes to you from the Lord,' said the attached card. The Lord may have sent me a magnificent new steam iron, but I guessed who had been His gloves.

3: I'm shy

It was the milkman who told me about Mr. Blake.

'Been took sudden in the night, poor old chap,' he remarked ghoulishly as he handed me my four pints. 'Nearly crashed me milkfloat into the undertaker's van, I did.'

I felt stunned. The Blakes were an elderly couple who had never had children and were deeply wrapped up in each other. I had managed a 'good morning' over their hedge, but that was as far as our relationship had progressed. I had no idea if they had any Christian faith. Poor Mrs. Blake. However would she be feeling now? Who would comfort her? The vicar and the doctor are paid to do that kind of thing, I told myself as I got on with the breakfast washing-up. Yet I kept on feeling that God wanted me to go round and see her that morning.

Shyness was the first item on my list of inadequacies. It had always been my greatest problem. I suffered agonies of self-consciousness when I had to walk into a crowded room or take my place in church.

'Mrs. Blake wouldn't want me barging in,' I argued miserably, but I could get no peace until I had popped out to buy her a card and a bunch of early daffodils. Whatever could I write in the card? My mind turned over hundreds of platitudes and scriptural references, but in the end I just said, 'We are all praying for you specially, much love from all the Larcombe family.' Then I set off down the road with my heart thumping.

God never makes mistakes in His timing, and only the day before a friend had lent me a tape which I had listened to while using my lovely new iron. I remember nothing about it except this, 'When you arrive at someone's house and you stand on the doorstep, make yourself feel conscious of the love of God flowing through you. Just switch it on like a current and let it precede you into the house or the strange room full of people. When you are not sure what to say to someone, just stand there and et God love them.' It had struck me at the time as being a very good cure for shyness.

The message of the tape was still clear in my mind as I walked up the neat path towards Mrs. Blake's door.

Just for once I was concentrating on God's love and not wondering what she would think of me, or how fat I looked in this coat. All the same as I reached for the bell I began to wish I was anywhere else in the world. Mr. Blake had only been dead a few hours, whatever did I think I was doing intruding like this? I was here because God wanted me to be, I told myself firmly, and with all my will power, I switched on that current of love and suddenly there in the doorway stood Mrs. Blake, her crinkled old face wet with tears. All the speeches that I had mentally practiced faded from my mind. I just handed her the card and flowers and gripped her hand.

'God bless you,' I whispered, and then turned and fled down the path – I had to, I was crying myself by that time. I felt such an idiot as I stumbled home. Fat lot of help I'd been. I'd only made a fool of myself.

It was several weeks later when I plucked up enough courage to ask Mrs. Blake round for a cup of tea, and it was then that she said suddenly, 'You know the day my husband was taken, and you came round with that card?' I mumbled vaguely through my biscuit crumbs.

'Well,' she continued. 'You never said anything, but you looked at me with such love, I felt peaceful all over. I've never forgotten that look in your eyes. I felt God sent you that day.'

Of course God *had* sent me, and it was His love that

she was responding to in my eyes. He had only used me as His gloves.

Listening as a cure for shyness

Mrs. Blake taught me still more about curing shyness. As the weeks went by, she badly needed someone to listen to her. She did not want me to do anything, nor did she want my advice or helpful suggestions. Just my time and my ears. The world is full of people like her who need to talk out their fears and anxieties, but most of us are too busy in our jobs or our work for God to spare the time to be an audience.

Jane also taught me that shyness can actually be an asset to God, although poor Jane herself has always found this difficult to understand.

'I feel useless to God,' she told me tearfully one day as we were waiting at the school gate for our children. 'Jim and I are such private people we feel paralysed by our self-consciousness. Wendy and Sue are always getting involved with people, and having crowds in their homes. They never stop talking about God. I've even heard them in the hairdressers and dentist's waiting room. I could never be like that.'

It is very easy for us all to fall into the same trap that Jane was falling into that day. We look at the way God uses someone else and we feel He must want to use us in the *same* way, but He knows we are all different so He uses us differently. Some people are delicate surgeon's gloves, while others are tough leathery gardening gloves. He needs us all for different jobs.

Sometimes these two friends of ours, Wendy and Sue, had caused me to feel overpowered by their strong personalities; while their tactless remarks and actions had often hurt. I loved them, they were my friends, but when I had a problem it was to Jane I would go. I could trust her never to repeat anything I said, while dear old

Wendy had once brought out a problem I had discussed with her in confidence, as an item for prayer at her house group! Jane could be trusted to pray, but she would never betray me. Wendy was always full of helpful advice. In fact, one could feel bowled over by her sheer bossiness. Jane never had enough confidence to offer unasked for advice, but talking to her helped me to see my life in proper proportion, and I realised myself what I should do. (Or was it that Jane prayed for me as I was talking?)

She may not have been very good at speaking to people, but she had no such inhibitions when it came to talking to God, and praying is surely the greatest thing we can do for anyone.

Jane thought of herself as being 'too sensitive', yet when other sensitive people needed a good cry it was to her that they gravitated, knowing that she would feel their sorrows deeply enough to weep with them, and not sit there telling them what they really ought to have done.

One of the worst things we can ever do while trying to reach people for God, is to preach at them. We need to earn the right to do that by little acts of kindness. Shy people seldom have the courage to preach, which must be an asset in itself.

Act the royal part – another cure for shyness

'I'm just no good at this kind of thing,' I wailed. 'I can't think why I let myself in for it in the first place.' My hands that were chopping mushrooms, were shaking so much it was a miracle I did not slice my fingers as well. The whole kitchen was littered with cookery books, expensive ingredients and my best bowls and dishes. We had decided to give a dinner party. Two new couples had moved into our estate, and we wanted to introduce them to two other Christian couples before we asked them if they would be interested in coming to our church.

Yet I seemed to have forgotten that the Bible demands us to 'Offer hospitality to one another without grumbling' (Peter 4:9 NIV). It does not say, 'if you feel it is your gift,' or 'if you are not shy.' It's a command, and we've got to do it without complaint! I was doing plenty of complaining that afternoon.

'This sauce tastes good anyway,' remarked my friend helping herself to a generous tablespoonful.

'Oh I don't mind the cooking part.' I told her. 'It's the entertaining I hate.'

'Pretend you're a princess,' advised my friend as she dipped her finger into a bowl of whipped cream. 'Look people straight in the eye and act the part until you believe it yourself.'

'I suppose if my father is the King of Kings, I really *am* a princess!' I laughed as I swept the mushrooms into the buttery frying pan.

That evening, as the doorbell rang or when I served out the veal chasseur, I kept mentally repeating, 'I'm a princess, I'm a child of the *King*.' Suddenly I did not feel all big feet and red ears any more.

Remembering just how important I am to God and how much He values me, has helped me through many an awkward situation, and nowadays people laugh when I tell them that I'm basically a shy person.

I honestly believe now that being shy and sensitive (so long as we don't use these traits as an excuse to do nothing) can actually make us more useful to God, because we have to depend on Him more in our helplessness, and we can understand better how other people may be feeling.

4: What if I don't feel loving?

One morning I was drinking a cup of coffee with my friend Sally. She admitted she was quite mystified about my 'new thing' as she put it.

'What do you mean God wants to love people through us?' she said, biting into one of her excellent homemade biscuits. I felt such a fool trying to explain that I felt like God's gloves.

'Well,' I replied awkwardly, 'it's not enough just to pray for someone who is ill. We should send them a card or go and visit them as well as pray. And it's no good sitting at home and 'loving' all the neighbours, without asking God who He wants us to demonstrate His love to that day. Perhaps He'll only want us to smile or chat over the fence, or He may want us to do someone's shopping if they are ill, or look after their child while they go to the dentist.'

'That's all very well,' retorted Sally helping herself to yet another biscuit, 'but what if you have neighbours like ours? We bought this house because it was cheap, but the people round here . . .! Well, you wouldn't want to know them, let alone love them. And besides,' she added defiantly, licking the crumbs off her fingers, 'I'm not a naturally loving person. Sometimes I feel I don't love my husband and sons, let alone the riff-raff in this road.'

I knew just what Sally meant. Love is not a natural emotion. On a bad day I often feel I don't love anyone much either. We are not inhuman monsters when we feel like this. We are changeable human beings like everyone else, and some of the people who God loves and brings to us for His practical care will positively revolt us. I discovered this painfully – soon after I began my first feeble efforts to reach out to the people in my district.

Making use of God's love

Three doors up the road from us, Jack and Pauline's marriage broke up. One day he went off with someone else and the break was final. Pauline was devastated, suddenly finding herself alone in the world with a child of two years old. I honestly believe that if she had been widowed it would have been easier for her to live through those first few months. At least she would have known that Jack had died loving her. Yet she had to face the cruel fact that he was still alive and working at the same job, wearing the jumper she had knitted for his birthday and going home at the end of the day to someone else. Not only did she have to cope with the devastation of being on her own, she also had to come to terms with her feelings of anger, rejection and bitterness.

'I just can't stand being in the house on my own,' Pauline sobbed as she told me how she felt, so she began to stay all day in mine. After a few weeks she seemed on the verge of a complete breakdown so she moved in with us and closed up her house. Many of my friends have happily shared their homes with other families and found the experience rewarding. So I felt very guilty when I found having Pauline constantly sitting round the house a real strain. In fact, to put it bluntly she began to 'get on my nerves'. So when she suggested that she went back to work I jumped at the idea. I felt I could manage her little boy far more easily when she was *not* there all the time. How wrong I was! The firm for whom she had previously worked gave her back her old job, and it was really the salvation of her self esteem, but coping with her child did nothing for mine! I had always thought I liked children, but not that little boy! It was not that he was noisy or naughty, he just revolted me. His nose never stopped running and he dribbled constantly from the corner of his big sloppy mouth. Then he caught chicken pox. Of course, it was not his fault, but he was completely covered with spots and I almost retched every time I looked at him. I knew this attitude was not good, but I disliked him so much I would not even pray about it.

One morning I was changing his nappy. The horrible spots covered his entire body and his nose ran more than ever. I looked down at this ugly little duckling and suddenly I new I had to cry out to God for help. These days the word love often means a sloppy emotional feeling, or a baser kind of lust. Yet the definition in my dictionary says: 'Love is an intense desire for another's highest good and happiness'. Love is not an emotion that always comes naturally to us. Sometimes it is a matter of our will and of making up our minds to love someone with God's love. All these thoughts raced through my mind as I washed him and dabbed calamine lotion on his spots.

'Please,' I prayed, 'I can't love this child, I don't even want to, but please give me your love for him and let me see him through your eyes.' The prayer was answered immediately. Something strange and supernatural happened to me in that moment. When I had put on his clean nappy I lifted him into my arms and really cuddled him. It was the first time I had even been able to do that, and he put his spotty little face down on my shoulder runny nose and all, and we stood like that, loving each other for a full five wonderful minutes. He and I became very special friends, but I still did not find it easy to live with Pauline. She just could not, or would not go back to her own house. Two women in one kitchen is a classically difficult situation. The strain began to tell on Tony as well as the children. Yet what could we do? Pauline seemed to need us and by coming with us to church she was beginning to know God as a reality in her life. If we pushed her out we might sour her relationship with Him. We told God how we were feeling, and almost at once He stepped in to help us. Pauline's firm offered her promotion in their branch which was in the town where her parents lived, and she moved into a flat in the road next to their house.

The danger of enthusiasm

Over the years I have always found that God never leaves people with us for longer than we can actually be useful to them or feel that we can cope with the pressures they bring. He seems to move them on to someone else at just the right time. However, that principle only seems to apply when we are doing something He really wants us to do. It is so easy to act on impulse in our own enthusiasm without first stopping to ask God if He really wants us to take on that particular task. We believe we are working for God and feel surprised and even 'let down' by Him if we find ourselves overloaded and our entire family under strain. A need does not constitute a call. It is not God's fault if we feel like that, because we never gave Him time to stop us from embarking on this enterprise in the first place.

That spotty little two year old is now a huge teenager, and every time I meet him I feel that strange surge of love which I know to be God's love. But He does not always give that love quite so immediately as I learnt to my cost some years later.

We had moved into a country village by that time, and I really do not think I ever hated anyone more than I hated Jemma – yes I really mean hate.

When I first met her I thought she was delightful and we often chatted as we met our children from playgroup.

She had a sweet little girl of two and a most attractive boy of four. Then one day the village rocked with the news that Jemma had decided to 'fulfil her potential – do her own thing', and she left her husband and those two lovely children, apparently without a second thought.

Because I was a registered childminder, Bill, who was quite distraught, asked me and another Christian friend to take turns in looking after the children while he was at work. Never have I seen two children change so tragically. The once laughling little girl withdrew from the world and would not be cuddled or played with, but sat all day facing the corner, rocking herself to and fro. Her brother went to the other extreme and became so viciously aggressive he was a danger to other children. Bill seemed to crumble and went to pieces completely. I can't remember ever really hating someone before, but I was so disgusted by what Jemma had done to three human beings, I literally did feel hate.

One morning I got a message to say that the children would not be coming to me that day because Jemma was back in the house to collect her belongings and wanted the children for one last day. I caught sight of her dropping them off at playgroup when I was delivering my youngest son Richard. All morning as I worked at home I fumed inside, tutting with outraged disgust, until suddenly God seemed to tell me to switch off the hoover and pray. As I knelt by the bed a strange thing happened. I knew He was speaking to me and He said 'I want you to tell Jemma I love her'.

'No way!' was my indignant reply as I switched the hoover back on again. 'Anyway,' I told myself, 'there'll be such a crowd of mums at the end of playgroup I wouldn't have the chance to speak to her alone.' For the rest of the morning I could get no peace. It was as if God was gently continuing to ask me to do this for Him.

'Well, Lord,' I said at last, 'if I meet her face to face

at playgroup, and she's all on her own then I will try to say it'.

Deliberately I arrived as late as possible and I was pleased to see the Scout Hut looked deserted when I got there. Just as I walked in at the gate, to my horror I saw Jemma coming out of the door. Not another mum was in sight. Here was my chance to speak to her, but I hated her, and I did not *want* God to love her, so I lowered my eyes and marched by her. When Richard and I were back in my car I felt rather guilty.

'Lord,' I prayed, 'if I see her on the way home, and it's easy to stop then I will tell her.'

I drove home the long way round feeling sure she would not push the double pushchair that way. But she did! I saw her just by a layby, and there were no other cars to be seen. I could easily have stopped, but I put my foot hard down on the accelerator and drove by without a wave.

As I cooked Richard's fish fingers my tears were falling into the pan and making the fat hiss. 'Lord,' I said, 'I really am sorry.'

'If you are sorry then you can still go,' He seemed to say. It was 3.30 in the afternoon when I finally capitulated, but by then it was much harder. I had to go right round to their house and knock on the door. Never have I felt such a fool! Jemma is a beautiful woman with the most enormous eyes I have ever seen.

'Jemma,' I stammered, 'God wants me to tell you that He loves you.' Huge tears filled her eyes and she seemed to crumple – suddenly I loved her because I was looking at her through God's eyes.

'I didn't think He ever could,' she sobbed. It would make a good story to relate that she became a Christian, went back to her husband and they all lived happily ever afterwards. But that's not the way it happened. She left with all her possession that night and I have never seen her again. But somehow I feel sure that she will never forget God is there loving her, and she will come to know Him if she has not already done so. The children settled and began to heal after many people had prayed for them, and now they are older things are much easier for Bill.

Perhaps we have to keep on remembering that 'God is always at work in you to make you willing and able to obey His own purpose' (Phil: 2:13 GNB). He actually makes us want to want what He wants! His love is like a huge reservoir that never dries up. It does not matter whether we are naturally loving by nature, because it is His love we are tapping, not our own.

In every church or community there are people who are very easy to love and care for. They seem to reflect back the love they receive. Dear old Winnie was just like that. I went to visit her in hospital just to give *myself* a treat. She was nearly ninety, but as she sat up in bed in her cuddly pink bedjacket, she looked as pretty as a teenager and her smile was so warm it would make anyone feel better.

'How wonderful of you to spare the time to come and see me dear,' she said, even though I knew she had received a constant stream of visitors all afternoon. 'I feel so surrounded with love I just don't know why you are all so good to me.' I knew *just* why, and I left the ward feeling cheered and happy; but secretly I knew I would not get my reward in heaven – I'd had it down here already.

It was a month later that I went to see Mrs. Whooster in the same ward. What a contrast! The minister had said from the pulpit on Sunday that she had been deeply upset because no-one from church had been in to see her in hospital. So it was only guilt that forced me to go. She sat up in bed nursing her afflicted stomach, looking for all the world like a shrivelled, bad tempered toad.

'What have *you* come for?' was her 'pleasant' greeting.

Her daughter had brought in the wrong nightie, her son had not bothered to come and see her (he lived in France!), the staff were rude and ill-trained, and as for the food . . .'

I staggered away at the end of twenty minutes hoping (unkindly) that her stomach would really be the death of her. Yet people like Mrs. Whooster need the love of God far more than the Winnie's of this world, who seem able to generate love wherever they go. When someone is difficult to love, our natural instinct is to give up and let them stew, but that is not God's way. It would be nice to report that my visits to Mrs. Whooster changed her completely, and she opened like a flower to God. Actually, she never seemed to change a bit and her stomach really was the death of her before too long.

5: *I'm frightened of becoming too involved*

One day I received a mysterious letter from the vicar. It said, 'I've had an idea, which I would like to discuss so I am calling a meeting for 8 o'clock on Thursday. Do come.'

I was still struggling with my shyness problem, but curiosity overcame me, and I went.

The room was full of all the church worthies. If you had been feeling mean you might say the 'do gooders'. The vicar opened the meeting with enormous enthusiasm. 'It has recently come to my notice,' he said, 'that in this parish there are people in great need of practical help. Only last week a social worker telephoned me and told me of an old man of eighty who has recently had a stroke. He is looked after twenty-four hours a day by his wife of seventy-four. She longs for someone just to commit themselves to going in once a week and sitting with the old man while she goes shopping. Many of you I know are already showing the practical love of God, but I feel we need to co-ordinate everything systematically. I would like to send a circular round to the whole district, giving everyone three numbers to ring if they need any kind of help. The people who answer the calls could then phone any one of us and we could leap into action.' His eyes positively gleamed 'They might be new to the district,' he continued 'and need someone to talk to, or they might be without a car and need a lift somewhere, or they could just be plain miserable and lonely.' He beamed happily round the crowded room, expecing us all to rally to his call, but it was at that moment that Elizabeth erupted. You could have cut the atmosphere in the room with a gateaux fork as she stormed to her feet.

'Vicar! Do you realise where all this could lead?' The vicar's face collapsed like a punctured balloon.

'We might have to be dealing with people who are having nervous breakdowns or terrible things like that.'

'Well, yes,' faltered the vicar, 'I expect we would.'

'But there are people who are trained and paid to cope with that sort of person,' continued Elizabeth. 'People like us wouldn't want to get involved with that kind of thing. After all we've got a Welfare State haven't we?'

The vicar was visibly daunted, but he continued as bravely as he could. 'Sometimes depressed people do feel very cut off from their neighbours, and a chat over a cup of tea is often a good back-up to the doctor's treatment,' he said.

'Well, I'm quite disgusted!' said Elizabeth and she swept out of the room, leaving a very deflated collection of people behind her.

As I walked home under the clear frosty sky, I discovered that I was shaking with rage. How dare Elizabeth be that uncommitted to the love of Christ? She was such a nice person too, I'd always liked her, yet her outburst had probably killed the vicar's 'Helping Hands' scheme before it had even been born. Why was I feeling so angry? I wondered, then it dawned on me. I was angry because Elizabeth had been honest enough to voice my own secret fears. Did I fear I too might be sucked into other people's lives and swamped by their problems? *Yes*! and I think many of us feel the same but I also feel that this natural reluctance and hesitation on our part can be an asset and not a failing. We have to recognise the fact that the people who live round us probably don't want to get involved with us any more than we want to be involved with them! Christians who barge into people's lives waving Bibles and spouting the answers to all their problems probably do untold harm. When we perform flamboyant acts of kindness for our neighbours they may well think we have some dark ulterior motive, or are trying to suck them into some weird new cult.

We must constantly be building bridges with people, but in a very natural and low key way. Simply to admire the roses in an old lady's garden, or even her hideous pug dog, might make it possible for us to help her six months later when she is laid up with a chest infection.

When Jacky's husband left her I longed to comfort her, but I had never had the opportunity to make any of these simple bridges. In fact, I had never even spoken to her. Her problems were private and she had no wish to share them with anyone else. I met her every afternoon at the school gate and I always tried to look friendly, but her tight lipped expression quelled me and made me frightened of being rebuffed. Then quite suddenly one evening she knocked on our door.

'Something uncanny is happening to me,' she said nervously 'and as you're the only person I know who goes to church I wonder if you can help me.' I can't think how she knew we went to church, but inwardly thanking God for hearing my prayers for her, I followed her back to her house because she did not want to leave her children alone.

'I sit here every evening,' she said when we reached her rather bleak sitting room. 'I try and watch the telly to take my mind off things, but my eyes keep being drawn to the bookcase, I can't stop them. I just keep looking at that Bible there in the middle. Some people called Gideons gave one to all of us when we left school. I never read it then, and I haven't touched it in years. Why do you suppose I keep having to look at it now?'

Of course, I was able then to tell her I thought it was God's way of showing her how much He loved her and cared about the way she was feeling. After that a huge barrier was lifted between us and she was able to talk to me at last about her hurts and fears.

A few weeks later I suggested her children might enjoy Sunday school as much as ours did, and soon she was coming along to church with us too. In the end she found God for herself, but I am sure that if I had rushed her, and pushed my way in too soon she would have recoiled, feeling I was intruding. My natural fear had prevented me from approaching her in my own strength. When we feel inadequate we are more likely to hand a person or situation over to God who always manages things very much better than we can.

Almost too late

On the other hand, when we feel God prompting us to do something however reluctant we feel, it is vital that we respond to Him immediately. My friend Sophie lives with the terrible knowledge that once she was almost too late.

'Somebody pointed out to me that a local girl, Sara Meyer was depressed and could do with a visit,' she told me. I changed the subject quickly because I just did not feel I had the energy to take on a lame duck just then. Two days later I was sitting at a parents' evening at my son's school, and a friend introduced me to Sara Meyer. We chatted for a while in the shallow way one does at occasions like that, but all the time I felt God prodding me into making a deeper relationship with this girl. But I stifled his voice and deliberately forgot about Sara.

A week or so later I unexpectedly had a free day – what a luxury. I had my hair done, took myself out to lunch and had a long window shop. Suddenly I arrived outside a florist shop and in the window was a large notice 'Show you care with flowers'. It struck me that I had used my day rather selfishly and perhaps I ought to buy a plant and go and visit some elderly member of our congregation. So in I went and as I waited to be served I prayed, 'Lord show me who I should visit.' As I was coming out of the shop clutching my cyclamen, I collided with the friend I had met at the school evening.

'Have you contacted Sara Meyer yet?' she asked. 'You know she's had three cancer operations don't you? I feel someone from church ought to befriend her, but I don't really feel I've got the time.'

That decided me. I had better give in and take my plant in Sara's direction, obviously God was trying to say something to me. Yet as I stood at her door, repeatedly ringing the bell I wondered why God had sent me to an empty house. I was just turning to go, when I heard a muffled noise from inside which startled me. Something made me try the door and I found it was not locked. I followed the strange sounds upstairs to the bathroom. Huddled behind the door clutching a bottle of sleeping pills was Sara. Her whole body was quivering with sobs. I almost carried her downstairs, made some tea and lit the fire in the cheerless sitting room. Holding her mug like a drowning man holds a rope, she told me that she had become so desperate with fear and loneliness, she had been sitting in the bathroom crying out to God to send someone to help her.'

'If He hadn't taken any notice, I was going to swallow the whole bottle of pills and finish with it all once and for all.'

Sara still has her problems, hang-ups and fears, and she is terminally ill, but Sophie takes her to church each week, and step by step she is leading her nearer to God.

6: What if I become a doormat?

I once attended a conference of the Dentists' Christian Union where I had been asked to give an address to the dentists' wives, and we discussed love in action. (I'm not suggesting that dentists or their wives need to learn this any more than the rest of us, that just happened to be our subject!) One girl came up to me after the discussion and said, 'It's all very well talking about all this caring for people, but I'm beginning to feel just like a doormat. We live on a large estate and anyone who wants to go shopping, or have their hair done, just dumps their kids on me. They know I never say 'no' and sometimes I have ten children there drinking my fruit juice.' (She might have added, 'and eating my kid's sweets', if she had not been the wife of a dentist!) 'People just say, "Oh, she's a Christian, she *ought* to do that kind of thing," so they take me for granted. Where do I draw the line between trying to love and care for people and allowing them to take advantage of me? Don't I have a right to a life of my own?'

We are dead

Actually, as Christians we don't have a life at all. We are dead people. Paul says in Romans 6: 6,11 (GNB) 'For since we have become one with Him in dying as He did, in the same way we shall be one with Him by being raised to life as He was . . . you are to think of yourselves as dead, so far as sin is concerned, but living in fellowship with God through Christ Jesus.'

47

Dead people have no rights, they own no property, in short they do not have a life of their own. That sounds horribly drastic and the first time I heard anyone say it I nearly jumped up and ran out of church. Tony and I had gone to hear Juan Carlos Ortiz from South America when he came to preach in Tunbridge Wells. We were both feeling very tired that night, but we hoped an evening out would do us good. We expected to be braced by the singing and soothed by a short address. Actually, we both felt as if we were sitting in an electric chair and we have never been the same since.

Juan Carlos said that when we *really* mean business with God and give ourselves to Him completely, we become as dead men and women. We have no home, it belongs to God. But He may let us go on living in it to take care of it for Him.

'An empty house is no good to God,' he thundered from the pulpit. 'He wants a cook and caretaker in there to look after the people He may want to send to His house for comfort and care. You don't have a car any more, it's God's car, but He needs a chauffeur for it to drive people about who don't have one. You don't have any money, it all belongs to God. It's not a question of giving generously to the church collection each week. You need to ask His permission before you buy a new suit with His money! You are just stewards for God, there to administer His possessions, learning to use them in any way He wishes.'

Tony and I had both given ourselves to God, but that is *much* easier than giving all one's possessions, and we were both stunned.

'If there is anyone here who really wants to serve God with everything he has,' finished this dynamic South American, 'I want you to stand up, take off your coat and tie it round your waist like an apron to show you mean to be God's servant, ready to look after his homes, cars and money.'

Feeling complete fools, we both stood up and did just that. It marked the turning point in our Christian lives.

I was so dazed I walked out of church with the crowd quite forgetting my handbag. Just as we were climbing into the car I said, 'Horrors darling! I've left my bag and all my money is there.' Tony burst out laughing.

'It's not your bag or your money now,' he said, 'it's the Lord's and I'm sure He is able to look after it.'

Was Jesus a doormat?

I wonder if the Lord's disciples would have acted differently if they had known that night in the upper room that the meal they were to eat together would be 'The Last Supper'. They had been arguing fiercely between themselves about who was going to get the top jobs in the new Kingdom of God that they expected would be set up at any moment. Not one of them wanted to do the menial job of washing the dust off every one else's feet. That should have been done by a servant if they could have afforded one.

Jesus wanted to demonstrate to them that no job in His Kingdom was to be considered more important than another. So He, the Creator of all things, 'took upon himself the form of a servant', by taking off his coat, tying a towel round his waist and kneeling down to wash their feet. John 13:13–14 (GNB) says, 'You call me Teacher and Lord, and it is right that you do so, because that is what I am. I your Lord and Teacher, have just washed your feet. You then should wash one another's feet'. Isn't He trying to tell us that He wants us to be willing to do anything for Him, even the most menial and undistinguished jobs?

In the Christian world today, I think we are still prone to believe that the great evangelists, apostles and ministers do far more for God than we do, and their jobs are of much greater importance than visiting a few old ladies who might not smell too nice. In God's eyes it is not important *what* we do for Him so long as we are faithful to Him in whatever He *tells us to do*. Of course, some jobs are much more ego-boosting than others We probably look at Paul and think he was one of the most illustrious Christians who ever lived, yet he says, 'We wear ourselves out with hard work . . . We are no more than this world's refuse; we are the scum of the earth to this very moment' (1 Cor. 4: 12–13 GNB). He obviously counted it a privilege to be a doormat or worse!

1 John 3: 16 (GNB) says, 'This is how we know what love is: Christ gave his life for us. We too, then, ought to give our lives for our brothers!' Giving our lives means holding nothing back. Was Jesus a doormat? Well how could the Creator of the very fibres from which doormats are made ever be demeaned by being one? But is there much difference between wiping someone's feet with a towel and letting them wipe their feet on you?

However, we are not the Son of God, just ordinary human beings who already have our lives fully committed. How do we cope when we have ten uninvited children drinking our orange juice, and feel so surrounded by people in need, we feel we will go under ourselves? Well firstly, we must remember Jesus felt like that too sometimes, and when He did He withdrew into a desert place to be alone. When He saw His disciples under too much pressure, He took them with Him for a rest. We are called on to be wise stewards not only of our possessions, but also of our time and energy. The Lord's servant is always more important than the services he might render. In His sight we are not doormats, but royal princes and princesses. I told the wife of that dentist to get alone before God and ask Him if He really wanted her to be a dumping ground. Maybe her kindness was being a real witness to her neighbours, and in time they would respond to the God that she served.

'Perhaps it's just my pride that is feeling "put on",'

she said. 'When we possess nothing it is God people are 'taking advantage of', not us. Perhaps the fact that I mind proves that everything *doesn't* belong to *him* yet.' Strangely, after she had talked all this over with the Lord, and given Him once again all her time, energy and fruit juice, we both came to the conclucion as we talked that it was neither safe or legal for her to be responsible for so many children, and she decided to explain this to the mothers while offering to have their children on specific, planned occasions.

It is vital that we always keep the initiative. Perhaps someone who is emotionally upset has been coming to your house and 'landing' on you at times when you want to be free for your family. Then learn to say firmly, 'let me come to you next time.' That way you can decide when to go and how long to stay.

When this panicky feeling of being overloaded hits us, *it is vital to pray about it* preferably with someone else, and not just to respond on an impulse.

Karen had only been a Christian for a very short time when her friend Kerry began to go through the trauma of divorce. Karen was her one support in a world that was crashing round her. At first, Karen burned with enthusiasm to help Kerry, but as time went on she began to resent all the time she was giving her. One day, Karen just exploded. She had not prayed about her mounting tension or discussed her feelings with a more mature Christian. She just told Kerry there and then that she did not want to see her again. The sudden withdrawal of friendship and support was too much for Kerry to take, and the following week she was admitted to the local psychiatric hospital where she spent the following three months.

We must remember that once someone who is emotionally hurt is trusting us for support and friendship, we can do untold harm to them by suddenly withdrawing it, just because we feel temporarily pressured.

It is better never to get involved with someone in the first place than to let them down when they need us.

That knowledge makes us all feel so inadequate that we could easily draw back into our shells, dreading that we might be lumbered with a parasite for the rest of our lives. As I have already said, I am convinced that when we have given to God everything we are and have He never allows us to waste our (His) time with someone when we reach a point where we can help them no longer. But how do we *know* when we have reached this point? This is the verse that always helps me here, 'trust in the Lord with all your heart and lean not to your own understanding. In all thy ways acknowledge him and he shall direct thy path (Prov. 3:6 AV). So often when we feel we have reached the 'end of the road' with someone, God just moves them on to someone else without our having to do anything about it. After all, He may want to bless someone else by giving them a chance to care for this person. Yet there are other times when He does seem to want us to take the initiative, and we shall only know when that time has been reached when we have honestly asked Him to tell us. When God has spoken to us it is unmistakable. There is no way to describe it, we just know that He has.

Yvonne came to spend a week-end, and was still with us over a year later. Every time anything upset her she took an overdose of sleeping pills or had major fits which the doctor told us were self-induced. We all loved her greatly, but suddenly one day while we were praying for her, Tony and I realised that we were not helping her by keeping her emotionally dependent on us. So we found her a dear little flat and supplied her with furniture and bits and pieces to make it cosy.

'I'll never cope on my own,' she wailed.

'But you won't be on your own,' we told her. 'The Lord will stay here with you all the time.'

'I'll try it out for a week,' she said, 'but don't be surprised if you see me back with my cases.'

'We're sorry,' said Tony very gently but firmly, 'if you *do* come back to us, we won't be able to take you in. You must learn to rely on God instead of us.' She burst into tears, and we left her in her new flat sobbing hysterically. I cried all the way home. 'She'll take an overdose,' I said, 'and we'll never forgive ourselves.' How we prayed for her that night! Next morning I had to fight my natural instinct to rush and see how she was. All day long we expected a phone call from the hospital telling us, as they had so often before, that she was in intensive care. No call came. This time was different because God had definitely told us to withdraw. She was twenty-nine and had never managed on her own before, but ten years later she is still living in her little flat. Coping on her own has so increased her self-esteem that she uses her home to entertain other people who need her. She runs the church library and spends several evenings a week reading to blind people. Sometimes when she rings me up and tells me about all the exciting things that fill her life, I tingle all over. When you see God working in someone's life like that it is one of the most exciting things that can ever happen to you.

We cannot be doormats if we don't see ourselves as doormats. Philippians 1:29 (GNB) says, 'for you have been given the *privilege* of serving Christ'. What higher calling could we possibly have, whatever job He gives us to do. We can be sure that He will never ask us to do anything that He was not prepared to do, and if we love Him can we dare to do less for Him than He did for us?

7: I don't have enough to share

It is no good pretending that it does not cost money to care for the people about us, and most of us live on a very tight budget these days. Cards cheer people up on all occasions but they do cost quite a bit, and to 'say it with flowers' leaves a huge hole in your pocket. Buying a Christian book for someone who is seeking God or even a modern translation of the Bible is a lovely thing to do, but costs mount up. Entertaining people for meals in our homes can drain the housekeeping, and even keeping the coffee jar replenished can be a nightmare. Where is all this extra money coming from?

That is the very question I asked Mrs. Stevens when she asked us round to dinner. I could not exactly thank her for the steam iron, even though I was pretty sure she had put it on my doorstep. I longed to know where she found the money for that kind of generosity.

She did not give us a straight answer at first, she just told us a story.

'When we had our first baby, and things were very tight for us financially, my husband bought me a perfectly lovely dress as a present. It was far more than he could really afford, but it was just a love gift. How I enjoyed wearing it, until one day a missionary came to stay. She had no nice clothes, and I could see by the way she looked at my dress that she liked it. She had weeks of deputation work ahead, and I felt if she had a lovely dress to wear her morale might be boosted as she had to face so many strange congregations. So with my husband's permission I gave her my dress. She was thrilled. About six months later things were even more difficult for us, because my husband was trying to set up on his own and I felt miserable that I had nothing decent to wear at all. Suddenly one morning I received a parcel. Inside was a dress almost exactly like the one I had given away. If anything, the colour was rather nicer. I never discovered who sent it to me, but I took it from the Lord. That kind of thing has happened to us countless times since then. The more we give away the more the Lord seems to give back again to us.'

She jumped up from the table, and producing a Bible she shoved the carrots and peas out of the way and laid it down in the place of honour. 'Look!' she said enthusiastically, '2 Corinthians 9:8 (GNB) promises us that "God is able to give you more than you need, so that you will always have all you need for yourselves and more than enough for every good cause". My husband and I have proved that time and time again,' she beamed. 'We have never been rich, but as we give to the people round us, it seems as if God faithfully gives back to us enough for our own needs and just a little over to share again. Of course, we must not be too extravagant or impulsive in our spending, but God is no man's debtor and when we have given to Him He gives back to us. Jesus Himself said "Give to others, and God will give to you. Indeed you will receive a full measure, a generous helping, poured into your hands – all that you can hold. The measure you use for others is the one that God will use for you" Luke 6:38 (GNB). If God wants us to have money to share with others, then it is surely up to Him to provide us with it.'

'Several times in our married life,' she continued, 'we have gone through patches when our money just did not seem to be going round. On each occasion we have been made aware of another couple in our church who has been going through even harder times. God has seemed to say to us, "Send them an anonymous gift". It seemed a ludicrously silly thing to do, but when we have done it, strangely our financial affairs have evened out and improved. Of course we don't give to God to get something out of it, but it just seems to work that way.'

Prov. 11:25 (GNB) seems to enforce this advice. 'Be generous, and you will be prosperous. Help others, and you will be helped.'

What about tithing?

Tony and I went home that night feeling a little confused. It had not been long since we had been to hear Juan Carlos Ortiz and we knew that we were only stewards of God's money now, and really had none of our own. All the same, whatever the Bible and Mrs. Stevens said, with three small children life was becoming a real financial struggle. Since before we had been married we had both practiced the biblical habit of tithing. That is setting aside a tenth part of all that we earned. We had put it away in a separate bank account, or even on some occasions, in the teapot on the mantlepiece! But when we realised that all our money belonged to God it had seemed pointless to keep this up, and the money we had once used specifically for God's work was soon absorbed by our everyday housekeeping bills. We both began to suspect that this was the reason why we were finding things so difficult financially – we were not being obedient to God, so we began to tithe again.

Some Christians believe that all their tithe should be given to their local church where the elders or Parochial Church Council can decide what to do with it. Of course, we have an obligation to support the church we attend, but I feel that some of that sacred money should be saved carefully so that when someone comes along in desperate need, we have a reservoir of readily accessible money with which to help them. It has never worried me when I use some of our tithe money to help buy food when I am entertaining for God. Of course, there are times when the Lord asks us to give sacrificially over and above our tithe. We've proved that what Mrs. Stevens said is really true and we never seem able to give more to Him than He gives to us.

He wants us all to give

When you don't have many of this world's goods, it is a great temptation to sit looking round the congregation in church and thinking, 'So and so have plenty, they ought to be the people to give, not us.' Yet God wants us all to use our money (His money) to share with our less well-off brothers and sisters. It was the widow's mite that gave Jesus more pleasure than all the gold coins the rich people threw into the treasury.

I heard a story once of a man who was listening to a sermon. The preacher said, 'If you have two houses, you should give away one.'

'Amen!' said the man enthusiastically.

'If you have two cars,' continued the preacher, 'you should give away one.'

'Amen!' shouted the man.

'If you have two coats, you should give one away,' finished the preacher. This time there was no enthusiastic response from the man in the pew, just an ominous silence. Of course, if we are rich we are able to share more with others, but that does not let the rest of us off the hook!

Does God want rich Christians?

We were having supper round our fire one evening with a highly enthusiastic young Christian.

'I think it's disgusting,' he said. 'There are several very rich people in our church. Why don't they sell what they have and help all the people in need?'

'Come down off the ceiling,' said Tony gently, 'and think where would the Christian world be without its rich Christians? Making and using money is a gift that God entrusts to some people just as He gives others the ability to preach or heal. God needs people to earn money for Him and money makes money. Where would the Missionary Societies be without them? Who would support full time Christian workers and build new churches?'

'Yes, but,' continued our young friend doggedly, 'surely Christians shouldn't live in huge houses with swimming pools in the garden?' I knew just which family in our church he was getting at, so I said, 'God uses the Jeffersons' house all the time. They are constantly reaching out to the people who live in a similar style – people who could not be contacted for God by other Christians.'

'Well I wish God would give me the gift of being rich!' said James stabbing his fork viciously into a roast potato.

'It's very easy to envy any gift that God has given to someone else!' laughed Tony. 'I often wish I was a great preacher or had a superb singing voice that I could use for God, but we just have to accept that God gives us all different abilities and assets. But God wants each one of us to be sharing what we have with other people and showing His love all the time. Of course, people can misuse their money and spend it selfishly, just as anyone whom God has entrusted with special gifts can use them for their own satisfaction.'

It is all very well to talk like that round a cosy fire, but not long afterwards Tony and I were to learn just how easy it is for Christians to suffer from inverted snobbery. We were asked out to dinner one evening by a couple who came to our church but not very regularly, and were very much on the fringe of things. Like the Little Oysters in *Alice in Wonderland* we 'hurried up all eager for the treat', but as we drew up in front of their house our courage failed us a bit. It was a positive mansion. We had a marvellous meal, lavishly cooked and served on bone china. It was exhausting just lifting the solid silver cutlery to our mouths!

'Oh dear,' I sighed on the way home, 'I couldn't possibly ask them back. Our house is so small and shabby, and I'm a rotten cook.' So we never did. I felt embarrassed about it, and so I avoided them on Sunday mornings. She must have thought me very rude, and a wall seemed to go up between us. Looking back over the years I feel a deep feeling of regret. Why couldn't I ask them back? *Pride*. For all I know they might have been very lonely, longing for a deeper relationship with us. I should not have minded that they had more material possessions than we had. We don't mind helping people who are less well-off, but our pride is affected when we are befriended by people who are richer than we are. As Christians we should be above that kind of thing.

Our homes belong to God. How dare we be ashamed of them? So many of us are prevented from practicing hospitality as the Bible commands us to do, simply because we feel we haven't got the right kind of furniture, we eat such plain food, or we can't possibly invite anyone round until we have done the decorating. But people need the shelter and peace of our 'God centered' homes *now*. In fact, if we wait until they are perfect we might make our visitors feel too stiff and formal to relax in them at all. Being a Christian does not mean putting on our best clothes and going to church, but allowing people to feel at home in our shabby homes, eat our 'ordinary' food and just be with us, and not the people we would like them to think we are. When will we ever learn that it is *us* people have come to see and not our perfect homes?

There is, of course, another side to this. Our homes may not be shabby, but so beautifully furnished and decorated that we hesitate to share them with people who might break or spoil things we feel are precious. I remember a beautiful set of Victorian dining chairs we had once, and the real pain it caused me to see a young man we had asked to a meal, roaring with laughter and flinging himself back in his chair, then the horrible crunch as the 130 year old mahogany splintered.

People do spill their coffee on our carpets, and drop our china when they help us to wash up. If they move in with us, they always seem to pickle the workings of the washing machine and drop the iron hot side down on the persian rug, and because we are human we mind!

Recently I heard someone say something that helped me a lot, namely that we have to hold all we possess in an open hand. Even if it does sound a bit trite to say, 'people matter more than things', it does actually happen to be true. Jesus said, 'Do not store up riches for yourselves here on earth, where moths and rust destroy, and robbers break in and steal. Instead store up riches for yourselves in Heaven . . . For your heart will always be where your riches are' (Matt. 6:19-21 GNB).

What happens to your home while you are on holiday? Rather than leave our homes standing empty, and praying that 'robbers won't break in and steal' have you ever considered offering another Christian family a free holiday while you are away? So many families just cannot afford holidays these days, but to stay in someone else's home may just provide a needed break in their daily routine.

Danger!

Certainly it is deeply rewarding to share all we have with other people, but we must always be ultra-sensitive to the effect our giving may have on the receiver.

When Marianne became a Christian, she was led to the Lord by a member of a well-off middle class church. Marianne lived in a very cramped council house and hated it. Her husband was an alcoholic which made it often dangerous for her to be at home because of his violence. The church was very loving and suddenly many homes were open to her – she looked so small and frail and had so many problems, people took her and her three small children right to their hearts. Soon Marianne was out every day spending her time in the beautiful and comfortable homes of her well-off sisters in Christ.

That went on for nearly two years. Then suddenly Marianne realised she was actually beginning to envy the people she so frequently visited. Accepting their constant gifts made her feel of less value as a person herself. Her husband had left her by this time, and she had allowed her garden to become overgrown, and her house was dirty and untidy. While she stood in her kitchen turning these thoughts over in her mind, a wise Christian friend tapped on her door, and when Marianne let her in, she could see by the concerned expression on her face just what she thought of the mess.

'I never seem to be here to give the house a good clean,' she said in answer to an unspoken comment. 'I've got so many friends, I prefer being in their houses.'

'But don't you realise,' said her friend gently, 'God has given you this house to use for Him? You ought to make it smile for Jesus.'

Marianne burst out laughing, 'smile for Jesus' seemed such a quaint thing to say. Yet that visit changed the course of Marianne's life. With the help of her many friends she did make her house 'smile for Jesus', and the Lord opened her eyes to all the less fortunate people who lived round her. Within weeks she had made a deep relationship with the girl next door, whose husband had also left her. Soon she had led her to the Lord and they found enormous enjoyment in each other's company. They both took part-time jobs at different times so they could look after each other's children. This did more for Marianne's self-esteem than all the gifts of money she had so often received in the past. She became a person in her own right, and not just 'poor little Marianne' whom everyone helped. Now she is known as a Christian by everyone on that estate, and people come to her when they are in trouble.

Of course Marianne needed all that love and spoon feeding in her spiritual babyhood, otherwise she might well have gone under to her problems, but thanks to the wisdom of the friend who visited her she discovered her own ability to care for people in her own right.

Postscript: One evening, one of the friends that Marianne had come to envy because she had a detached house on a private estate (with a downstairs loo and a double drainer sink unit) was standing in her kitchen gazing like old Mother Hubbard into her embarrassingly empty fridge. She had exactly 10p in her purse, and in five minutes her four extremely hungry children would be coming home from school, and a half a loaf of bread and a tin of soup would not go far to fill their hollow legs. The reasons why she had run so short are not important, but she told me that few things have touched her more than the sudden appearance of Marianne with two pounds of sausages in a bag.

'I suddenly felt I was supposed to bring you these,' she said shyly and then rushed away to her school cleaning job.

'Those sausages tasted like rump steak!' confessed 'Mother Hubbard'.

8: *I haven't the time*

By now I feel sure some readers will be panicking. Of course you long to be God's gloves and do anything He asks of you, but your time is already heavily committed. If your children are small you are on duty twenty four hours a day. Your career may be very demanding, leaving you little time for the ordinary chores of life. You could be responsible for elderly parents and already have a full church life, and your mind boggles at the thought of fitting anything else in. Does God want you to do even more?

We all realise that our time belongs to God just as much as do our material possessions, yet it is often hardest of all to be a good steward of this most precious commodity. Each day consists of hundreds of small jobs, some of which we have to do, while others fall into the optional category.

Suppose it is seven in the evening – you've had your meal and hope to go out to a church meeting at eight. Do you: Pull a few weeds from the garden? Read a story or play a game with your small son? Ring your recently widowed mother? Pop next door and see if your lonely old neighbour needs anything? Have a shower and wash your hair? Drop into your 'local' and get to know your neighbours in their territory? Write a letter to a sick friend, or simply put on the telly and relax? This hour belongs to God, but how do we know how He wants us to spend it?

Of course we shall never know how God wants to be served unless we take the time to get to *know him person-*

ally. Although all our time belongs to Him, He still longs for us to reserve a little patch of our day when we can give Him our undivided time. At certain stages of our lives that is easier than others! If you have several small children crawling all over you night and day, ten minutes alone with God is a vast achievement; but we are not *only* in communication with Him as we kneel down by our beds, and we need to develop the habit of visualising Him with us, whatever we are doing. It is perfectly possible to chat things over with Him as we travel to work or peg out the washing. We may not be able to talk to Him while we are typing or filing letters, but we can enjoy the fact that He is watching us, and we can thank Him for the lovely things He has made as we take the dog for a walk or watch the nature programmes on T.V.

I remember one very pressured time in my life when I felt convinced that I was trying to help various people, but never finding time to pray for them. So I devised a system of sticky labels with coded names on them. I stuck one on my overworked washing machine, and every time I pushed the dirty clothes through the port-hole it reminded me to pray for a family who had lost their teenage daughter. Another was over the bathroom sink helping me when I cleaned my teeth to pray for a girl who was having a nervous breakdown. Other people had their turns while I peeled the potatoes or opened the fridge. Fortunately, they never recognised their names!

Priorities

It is vital to remember that He wants us to be *whole* people with our priorities in the correct order.
1. God first.
2. If we are married our families come next. (See chapter on Families at Risk.)
3. Love your neighbour as yourself (Luke 10:27b). It is

difficult not to feel vaguely guilty about loving ourselves just as we love other people, and yet actually we owe it to God to spend time each day on ourselves. The Bible tells us that He actually lives in us, making our bodies His temple (1 Cor. 6:19). Our sacred job is to maintain that temple and keep it looking and functioning as well as possible. That means taking time to exercise, eat the right food, relax, sleep and keep our hair and clothes looking neat and clean.

Loving our neighbour includes every kind of 'Christian work' we could ever do, as well as our attitude to every human being we meet.

4. The Bible constantly emphasises the importance of doing our job of work as carefully and conscientiously as possible. God loves order, you only have to look at the universe to realise that. So being His gloves never gives us an excuse for producing shoddy work, being a lazy employee or casual about our responsibilities.

These may be our priorities, but with God's help we have to keep the balance right. If we become a workaholic, excessively house proud, spend all our spare time developing our physical fitness and good looks, live too long in the aesthetic world of music, books and the beauties of nature, or even become so absorbed in our family that the rest of the universe does not exist for us, then we are squeezing out of our day the time we could have been spending on other people. Sometimes it is a good idea just to stop crashing madly round for five minutes and consider just how we do spend our time.

Once I had a rather nasty shock. I was asked to go and speak at a coffee morning for Christians on the subject of *time*. I felt so pressured and overworked myself just then, I thought it might be safer if they did the talking! So I devised a chart for them to fill in which I hoped would promote discussion and show in detail how they all divided up their time each day. Before going I thought it would be only fair for me to fill it in myself, and I was horrified to discover how much time I actually wasted.

I did a quick time and motion study on my routine and discovered with a little forethought, that I could easily pick up five minutes here, and with a bit of reorganisation another ten minutes there, and was I really spending that long watching T.V.? In the end, I thought that if I got up fifteen minutes earlier in the morning I might even get everyone out of the house by 8.30 am without screaming at them like a demented market trader. I set off for the meeting next day feeling rather a fool. I don't know if anyone else was blessed that morning but I certainly was, my only difficulty was stopping them from talking at the end!

'It is vital to make two lists every morning,' I remember one woman saying. 'The first list is for jobs that *must* be done. The other one is for things you could do if you don't get interrupted.'

'A job always expands into the time we allow for it,' said another wise sage. 'If we learnt to speed up the jobs we *must* do, we could leave more time for the things we *could* do.'

'The first thing I do on waking,' added a third, 'is to put the whole day in to the Lord's hands, and I ask Him to show me just how He wants me to live through it. Then if I don't get everything done that I've planned to do, I don't get hassled.'

After hearing that talk which I never actually gave, I realised I did have more time for the outside world than I ever thought possible. but it was not until later that I discovered the secret of time sharing.

It was snowing hard, one January day but I didn't care. I wasn't going out. I had planned one of my 'feed the freezer' cooking days and was thoroughly looking forward to it. I loved baking in bulk, and had borrowed some sermon tapes from church to listen to while I worked.

No sooner had I lit the oven and tied on my apron when I heard a thump on the back door. I felt irritated. If I was to accomplish all I had planned to do before the children came home from school, I had no time for interruptions. Unfortunately for me, the kitchen door was glazed and it was no use pretending I was out. On the door step, looking rather like a snowman, stood a tramp. He was well known in the district and during the summer he did odd gardening jobs, but the winter was a cheerless time for him sleeping rough in barns and sheds.

As I opened the door, and saw his shabby clothes which smelt rather unpleasant and his waterlogged boots, I suddenly realised that Jesus really loved that man, and had sent him to me for shelter.

'Come in,' I said still rather unwillingly. 'I'll make you a cup of coffee.' I noticed his shoulders relax and a look of relief spread over his unshaven face.

'I hope you don't mind if I get on,' I said. 'I'm a bit busy today.' Far from minding, he seemed to be delighted.

'I haven't smelt hot cakes since I lost my dear wife,' he said, and from nine in the morning until three, he never once stopped talking as he sat in the armchair in the corner of the kitchen, his damp clothes steaming from the warmth of the radiator. Even the necessity of sampling every goodie as it came out of the oven and swallowing numerous cups of coffee never seemed to halt his flow.

'Really?' I said as I tried to read my cookery book, and 'Whatever did you do then?' as I peered at my scales. My brain felt sore and my ears were battered by the story of his life. But when the snow gave way to a watery afternoon sun and his natural restlessness exerted itself, he said with tears in his eyes as he shambled out of the door, 'Thank you for letting me say all that. It's been the nicest day I can remember.' I felt very small as

I watched him shuffling away through the snow. To have someone to talk to had been his greatest need, and I had resented missing my sermon tapes. He had not actually taken up any of my time. He had only shared it.

When I was first married, the advent of a visitor meant that I had to clean and tidy my house meticulously before they arrived. If they were coming for coffee I had to bake homemade biscuits, and when people came for a meal in the evening the preparations took me the entire day. I felt visitors required my undivided attention. Since then, however, I have discovered that few people want to be treated like that. They would really rather share our lives. A recently widowed friend of mine told me that she found one of the worse parts of bereavement was the long lonely evenings watching T.V. by herself. When a neighbour asked her to pop in each Wednesday evening so they could watch a particular serial together it made all the difference to her week.

Stephen was deeply concerned about his friend Roy who had just been made redundant only a few months after losing his wife.

'I hate to think of him stewing through this heat in that tiny flat in town with a six year old under his feet all day,' Stephen said to his wife.

'Why don't you ask them for a week's holiday?' she suggested. 'The little girl would love playing with our kids, and the country air would do them both good.'

'Roy would never come,' replied Stephen. 'He'd think we were dishing out charity.' But as he prayed for Roy he had a sudden idea. 'I've come to ask a huge favour,' he said, banging on Roy's door one evening. 'I'm taking next week off to decorate our lounge and dining room, but I hate hanging paper, and I was wondering if you'd stay over with us and give me a hand. Tess will keep an eye on your girl.'

Ten days later when the work was finished the two men sat surveying their handiwork and celebrating with a cup of tea. Through the open window came the sounds of happy children's voices, and suddenly Roy said:

'You know this has been the happiest week we've had for more than a year.'

It had actually saved Stephen time to have Roy with him. Lynne finds the same thing. Each Thursday she gives her whole day to Nardia, a friend who is struggling through a mental breakdown.

'I could never spare anyone a whole precious day on a regular basis,' says Lynne, 'I'm far too busy, but I always make my bread on Thursdays, and Nardia seems to enjoy helping me. I save jobs like making chutney or jam for that day, and when her hands are busy she seems to find it easier to talk. I'm sure if I just sat and listened to her she would dry right up.'

I used to live practically next door to Andrea, a very special friend who is as disabled as I am now. When we moved ten miles away we both realised our chances of seeing each other were slight. Then another friend, Kay, realised our plight. Every two weeks she comes into town for a major shop-up, and on the way she picks up Andrea and deposits her at my house which is conveniently near the shops, fetching her on the way home. Doing this does not actually take Kay's time, it only took perception, but it means more to the two of us than we can ever express.

Of course, if we are going to go out and visit someone who is shut up in their home or in hospital, then it will take time which has to be generated by extra efficiency or sacrifice. That really leads us back to the dilemma of 'How do we really know what God wants us to do next?'

I got a lot of help on this point from my friend Madge who is probably one of the busiest people I know. She too starts her day by making a list as she sips her early morning tea, but she also prays 'Lord please take control of the telephone and doorbell so I do not have more people than I can cope with for you, and Lord let me always be in the right place at the right time.'

'One day my list of jobs seemed even longer than usual,' she told me, 'and I really began to feel pressured as I dashed round trying to get through them all. One of the items on the list was "Go to the Missionary prayer meeting," but I really didn't want to go. How could I work up a burden for South America when the kitchen was full of Saville oranges waiting to be made into marmalade and my roses were crying out to be pruned on the first fine day we'd had in weeks? So I just flopped down at my kitchen table and prayed "Lord where do you want me?" All through the busy morning I kept feeling certain I should go to the prayer meeting so very reluctantly I left as late as possible and found myself sitting in the back row next to someone I had never met before.

'What am I doing here?' I kept asking myself as I listened to other people praying and remembered my marmalade and roses. 'I need not stay for the inevitable tea and biscuits at the end,' I told myself, and was just going to sidle quickly towards the door when I realised that the woman sitting next to me would then be stranded in our row without anyone to talk to, and she looked rather like a fish out of water.

Very reluctantly I started up a perfunctory conversation, but soon realised that she had only been to church a couple of times and had come to the prayer meeting 'to see what happened at one'. Bit by bit, it dawned on me she was really seeking God.

'All you people here seem to have something extra that I don't understand,' she said.

'It's not some*thing*, but some*body*.' I beamed. 'She came back to my cottage and we sat talking by the fire for ages. Over the next few weeks she gradually began to know the *somebody*, and earlier this year she was confirmed. What a lot I would have missed if I had stayed behind to prune the roses.'

'My times are in thy hand' (Psm. 31:15 AV) (but only if I put them there!)

9: *I never seem to be successful*

Julie was the first person I asked for help when I started to try and write this book. If anyone has ever been used as God's gloves, Julie has. Over the last twenty years we have developed a very deep friendship even though our personalities are poles apart. While I am shy, Julie is amazingly gregarious and loves having people round her all the time. God has really used that natural trait and over the years her home has been a safe harbour for countless people. Whole families have stayed with her for months, her children's security has never seemed threatened and her serenity has never been rocked, while I would have been tearing my hair out. She possesses the enormous gift of making everyone feel they are the most important person who has ever entered her house. When she says goodbye, she never shuts her door leaving you with the feeling that she is rushing back to all the jobs you have prevented her from doing. She always walks right down to the end of her little driveway and waves the car right out of sight. A small gesture perhaps, but it conveys so much.

Julie was rather reluctant to tell me about the many people she has helped over the years, and I had to ply her with countless cups of coffee before she could get herself started, but when she finally began to talk, my heart sank.

'You make it all sound so easy,' I wailed. 'Someone moves into your road, you befriend them, and in no time they and their husbands are baptised members of the church. It hardly ever seems to happen to me like that.

I might love and care for someone for ages, but often when I start talking about the Lord, a shutter comes down and they don't want to know. What do I do wrong? Or was I just born unsuccessful?'

'Who said you had to be a success anyway?' demanded Julie. 'God only asks us to be obedient. I've picked out the success stories, but the great majority of people I love for God don't end up "happily ever after." So often we want to see instant results, everyone must be healed, employed and converted within months of knowing us, and when they don't make the progress we expect, we drop them, leaving them bewildered and worse off than before. Christians sometimes go all out to make a friendship with someone, but there are strings attached to their love, and when the person does not come along to church or the wives group, that friendship is withdrawn. God sometimes seems to move very slowly and He often wants us to give people room to be themselves and find their own identity. They often feel inadequate as people and it is our job to build them up. Showing them how much we care for them will help them realise how important they are to God – but the process may take years.

Our G.P. put me in touch with a girl who suffered from agoraphobia. She just did not dare to go out. I spent hours of every week with her, gently helping her to cope with her feelings of panic, and bit by bit she began to be able to go into shops with me or ride on the bus. After what seemed like an eternity to us both she could do these things on her own, and now she is living a full and normal life. She knows I'm a Christian, but she has never shown any interest in spiritual things herself. Sometimes I'm tempted to feel I wasted all that time, but then I tell myself it was God's time I was using not mine. He may have plans to bring her to Himself much later in life.

Billy Graham feels on average someone has to be in contact with seven different Christians before they commit their life to Christ. The Christians are like links in a chain, all equally important, yet so often only the last link feels successful.'

'Sometimes just a chance remark can work like a link,' I agreed, and went on to tell Julie of a friend I have who knew nothing of God when she was married. Her first baby was desperately ill when he was born and was whisked into the Special Baby Care Unit. Eve was on her way down from the ward to see him and she was crying in the lift. A nurse was standing next to her.

'I can see you're sad,' she said gently putting her hand on Eve's arm, 'why not try praying about it?' The doors of the lift opened and they never met again, but those words were seared into Eve's mind. She felt she could not pray if she knew nothing about God, so as soon as she could, she went to church for the first time ever, and began to read every Christian book she could lay her hands on. Other Christians helped her faith to grow and she is now one of the most wonderful Christian women I know, having led countless other people to God. That nurse will not know until eternity just how much her words were used. She was just a link in a chain.

As Julie laughingly remarked when she heard this story, the poor girl probably went to bed that night thinking she had done nothing for God all day!

Personal rejection

'Do you ever find you get really hurt by other people?' I asked.

'Yes of course I do,' Julie replied looking down into her coffee cup. 'You meet someone, perhaps at church or the school gate, and invite them into your home, praying it will be a safe environment in which they can find God. But as soon as they feel they are getting too close to Him, they take off in a cloud of dust, and if you have given them lots of your time, love and even material things you can feel very discouraged and rejected. "What's the point?", Satan whispers, "Obviously God hasn't given you a gift of helping people in this way." We just must not listen to him, and keep on remembering God gave people a free will to accept Him or turn away. After all, not everyone who was healed or fed by Jesus or who heard Him speak, followed Him. I think realising this fact is what helped us to come to terms with our feelings about Phil. That episode was one of the most ghastly experiences of my life,' added Julie ruefully.

When things go wrong

'Phil was in his twenties when he first turned up at our church. Quite obviously he had emotional and personality problems, and our hearts just went out to him. He had no family or friends and began to spend nearly all his spare time in our house.

Over the next three years we treated him as one of the family, he even came on holiday with us, and we never had a weekend without him. He was always just on the point of finding God, but always something seemed to hold him back. Then suddenly everything went wrong. He fell deeply in love with a girl who often visited us, but when she told him she didn't love him in a romantic way, he took all his fury out on me.

It was a Saturday morning and he must have been watching the house, because as soon as he saw David's car drive off he walked through the front door. We never locked it, and he had been coming in and out like that for three years. The children were watching T.V. and I was upstairs making the beds. He walked straight upstairs and suddenly without warning, he attacked me.

I was punched and kicked, had my hair pulled and my thumbs bent backwards. I was terrified that if I cried out, the children downstairs would hear, come up and maybe he would turn on them, so I bit my lip and prayed desperately. It seemed like hours, but it was probably only minutes later that I heard David's car pull into the drive again. I was so winded by this time I could not have shouted but fortunately he walked straight up stairs, took in the situation at a glance and marched Phil out of the house.'

'Was that the last you heard of him?' I asked with a shudder.

'No,' she replied sadly. 'That happened ten years ago, but we still get abusive letters from him, and nasty phone calls. It took me ages to come to terms with why God had allowed that to happen. But you see, we realised we were only sharing (as the Bible puts it) 'the fellowship of His sufferings' [Phil. 3:10 AV]. Jesus loved people, offered them so much, but yet "He came unto His own and His own received Him not." Judas Iscariot lived with Him for three years too, and then betrayed Him. People will treat us in the same way as they treated the Master. When we help people it is not what we do for them, or our prayers that count. It is God who is reaching through us to them, and He is the one who is ultimately glorified by their acceptance of Him and His healing in their lives. The Lord's servant is not called upon to be successful, just faithful.'

10: Danger! Families at risk

It can be desperately frustrating to feel a deep desire to help the people around you, and use your home for God and yet to be married to someone who does not share or even understand this desire. You can either:

1. Breathe a heavy sigh of relief and feel, 'all that caring would be alright if I were single, but obviously I'm not called to that work'.
2. Find ways of caring for people that will not inconvenience your partner.
3. Just start inviting people into your home and hope her or she will get used to it.

We were once asked out to a meal where the wife was obviously trying to follow the latter course of action. It was ghastly. The husband, although a keen Christian, was completely unable to relate to people, and he obviously resented our being there at all. Halfway through the meal, they had a whispered row in the kitchen and the whole evening was so uncomfortable I hate to remember it. Had we been seeking God, or needing to talk over some worry with them, we could never have done so, and if the object of the evening was just to have a happy time of Christian fellowship, then that certainly was not the outcome. We can allow God to cure our own shyness, but we cannot force someone else out of their shell unless they are ready and willing.

Even in a Christian marriage, one partner can sometimes feel unsure of being really loved, and therefore find it hard to share any love or even attention with other people. Sometimes, this is merely a temporary state caused by outside pressures or poor health.

Paula really enjoyed her life and found it deeply fulfilling. Her husband Gerry was a firm's rep and spent all the week away travelling. Paula's sons were teenagers so she enjoyed a great deal of freedom which she used in God's service. Every Wednesday she had a tea party in her home for the older members of her church. When any of them were ill, Paula cared for them and she was always on hand to run them into town for hospital appointments or special shopping excursions. Then one day Gerry came home, white and shaken. His firm had collapsed and he had been made redundant.

A month later Paula came to see me, and suddenly burst into tears over coffee.

'I just don't know what to do,' she sobbed. 'Poor Gerry, I feel so sorry for him, there don't seem to be any jobs in the offing and he just sits round the house all day long. He wants me to be with him twenty-four hours a day. He seems to resent my old people and calls them "pet dogs". I've given up the Wednesday teas, but he even made a fuss when I popped out to see Mrs. James who is in bed with bronchitis. I know he's always been a shy man, but I just cannot understand this selfishness.'

We had always liked Gerry immensely, but we also realized he was a very insecure man. Paula was the pivot of his life, and losing his job had awoken in him many insecurities.

'Gerry needs you,' I said gently, 'you will have to trust the Lord to find someone else to care for these old people – at present he needs all your love, time and energy.'

Gerry was unemployed for three long years, but gradually through that time he came to know God better. This greatly increased his feeling of self-worth. He and Paula used to pray together each morning after the boys had gone to school, and soon Gerry was joining Paula in her prayers for the people who lived round them. His prayer began to be converted into action, and soon they were working together caring for their neighbours. One day another church member asked Paula, 'How are all your "pet dogs"?' Gerry nearly jumped at the man.

'How dare you call them that,' he said fiercely, 'they are people who God loves and Jesus died for!'

That story had a happy ending, but that does not mean that all stories will. It can be particularly hard for people whose married partners do not understand their commitment to Jesus Christ. Fiona was already married to a Muslim when she became a Christian. Because she is British, Hassan grudgingly concedes that her faith is important to her, and allows her to attend one church gathering a week. That means an agonising choice between morning or evening worship or her house group evening. Fiona longed to serve the Lord in some definite way, and would have loved to be a Sunday school teacher, but that would have meant a Tuesday evening of prayer and preparation.

'What can I do for you, Lord,' she prayed in her frustration, 'that won't upset Hassan?' Then she realised that although her husband expected her to be there to wait on him hand and foot when he was at home, during the day when the children were at school she really did have time for God, provided she speeded up her housework and gave up her passion for reading novels. She developed an extraordinary knack of always turning up at the homes of other church members at just the right moment. If anyone was in any kind of crisis through family illness or bereavement, she would arrive saying, 'I'm not here to talk, so give me a job or I'll go.' Her minister's wife told me 'Whenever I crawl in exhausted from speaking at the Women's group or I'm tied up counselling someone, Fiona seems to just arrive and take my little boy for a walk or wade through the ironing. She makes it possible for me to do much more for God.' Hassan has no objection to her visiting friends, and he never bothers to ask how she spends her days.

Couples who are not in complete spiritual harmony have another problem besides the use of their home and time – their money. It can be maddening for a wife to see her Christian husband giving or lending money to someone else when she feels it should have been spent on new curtains or a holiday.

Sybil was married to a very wealthy man who was not a Christian. He never begrudged her spending money on herself, but he was livid when he discovered she had bought a friend a new washing machine.

'After that experience,' she told me, 'I started earning money by drawing portraits of people's dogs and cats. The money was really mine to share, and meeting the people gave me lots of chances to talk about God.'

The wonderful thing is that even if our partner makes it difficult for us to be used as God's gloves for other people, nothing can stop God from using us to love our neighbours, and this is just what my friend, Mrs. Stevens taught her neighbour Pearl. She had led her to the Lord just a few weeks before by many little acts of practical kindness. Now they were both praying together regularly for Pearl's husband Dave.

Pearl so admired her spiritual mother that she tried to model herself on Mrs. Stevens's example and began a positive explosion of caring, but because she possesses enough enthusiasm and energy to drive five women, she went rather too far!

'It's so wonderful,' she gushes as she sat one morning drinking coffee in Mrs. Stevens's kitchen. 'God is really using my nursing experience. I am out all over the town caring for people now.' She was prattling on, hoping to impress Mrs. Stevens, and she did not notice the latter's dangerous silence. 'Dave is getting quite jealous,' she giggled. 'I'm sure he thinks I'm having an affair.'

'And aren't you?' enquired Mrs. Stevens ominously.

'Well you know I'm not,' replied Pearl indignantly. 'I'm working for God.'

'But look at it from Dave's point of view,' said her wise neighbour. 'You *have* fallen in love with someone else – God, and Dave may be feeling very pushed out. I've seen him trailing home from the London train, so tired he's hardly able to walk, and I know you are not in the house to welcome him home because the car's out. You say you want him to become a Christian . . .'

'Oh, I do!' exclaimed Pearl. 'More than anything.'

'Well, if I may say so, you're going about it in exactly the wrong way. You should be directing this loving energy towards Dave, and not away from him. *Love* him to Jesus.'

With Pearl there are no half measures, and Dave told us later that he really did not know what had hit him!

'Pearl's never been what you might call the easiest person to live with – up and down and hard to please, but suddenly she changed into the most wonderfully loving wife a man could ask for. I got my favourite food cooked to perfection, my trousers pressed, socks darned, she almost ironed the newspaper!' Dave had watched his brother and sister-in-law 'becoming religious' and altering radically, and when his wife changed as well, he just could not stand out against God any longer and soon he too was a Christian.

Dave and Pearl began loving people in partnership and are now giants in their own church. Without that wise advice, Pearl's enthusiasm might well have driven a wedge between them, or made it impossible for Dave to find God himself.

What about the children?

The Palmers had none of the problems we have just been discussing. They work together as a perfect team and are universally popular in their church. 'They would do anything for anyone' is the impression they give. Their teenage son is a friend of our oldest boy Justyn, and one day when he came to supper he suddenly said, 'The trouble in our house is, Mum and Dad are so busy looking after everybody from church, they don't have time for us any more. You would have to have a nervous breakdown,' he added bitterly, 'to be noticed in our home.' The tragic thing was that a year later he did have a nervous breakdown and he's not better yet.

I wonder what it might feel like to be a child in an 'open home'.

Your mother has nagged you to tidy your room before school – well it's not really your room, you're having to share with your brother because your own room is needed for a girl who has nowhere else to live. She worries you a bit because she moans a lot in the night and talks to your parents about disturbing things you don't really understand. You work hard on the tidying, and go off to school feeling pleased with yourself. You can hardly wait to get home at the end of the day because you've heard there's going to be a school trip to France, and you want to ask if you can go. But when you burst in through the back door a strange woman is crying in the kitchen, taking all your Mum's attention. She has a kid of about two and you can see it through the window fiddling with the catch on your rabbit hutch. You try and complain to its mother, but you are told to go and watch telly.

As you go upstairs to change a horrible sight meets your eyes. That kid must have been pushed up into your room to play and give his mother peace to cry. All your possessions are scattered everywhere. Why ever did you bother to tidy them this morning? The leg is wrenched off your action man, and you kick the remains of him across the room in a rage.

No sooner are you settled by the telly, when the door-bell rings. A young man with long untidy hair comes in.

He smells rather, but as Mum can't cope with him and the other woman she shoves him in the sitting room with you. He sinks down into your Dad's best chair and a deep gloom settles over the room. He doesn't much care for the children's programmes and asks if you mind changing channels. You do mind, but Mum says visitors come first, so you wander out to see if your rabbit has survived. Thank goodness the crying woman and her detestable young are leaving. You're starving hungry by this time and so is your big brother who is home now and taking his bad temper out on you. Mum starts cooking tea but she's so distracted, trying to talk to the long haired man at the same time, as well as answering the phone that your fish fingers are burnt and the chips are soggy. It doesn't really matter though, because you feel a bit sick now – the man smells so horrid. Thankfully you see Mum giving him all the money in her purse and off he goes. Now's the chance to ask about the French trip.

'Darling,' says Mum, 'we couldn't possibly afford it.'

'Of course you couldn't,' you think bitterly remembering the man sticking Mum's money into his dirty coat.

'Never mind,' you comfort yourself, tonight it's your favourite T.V. programme and you and Dad like to watch it together. No sooner are you both comfortably settled, than the doorbell rings yet again.

'My husband's walked out,' someone wails in the hall, and Dad and Mum are soon both fussing round. The T.V. is switched off and you and your brother are sent up to bed early.

Of course, that story is fictitious. But the sad fact remains that the caring urge of some parents have actually damaged their own children to the extent that *they* need the constant care of others in later life.

If we are blessed with children, then we must realise that after God and our marriage partner, they are our priority, and their spiritual welfare is more important than anything else we can do for God. They are with us and need us for such a short time. They are grown up and gone before we realise it. Of course, I am not saying that all the time we have our children with us we must not share our lives with anyone else. That would rob our children of many vital things.

1. They would not see God's power at work in changing people's lives.
2. They would not learn the biblical principles of hospitality and sharing.
3. The tolerance of God would not be demonstrated by our treating a tramp with as much deference as a prosperous businessman (James 2:1–4).
4. They would not realise the joy of 'entertaining angels unawares'.
5. With our constant, undivided attention they would probably grow up horribly self-centered and would feel so smothered they might want to leave home at the earliest possible moment.

All these lessons, however, can only be learnt when a child knows for sure that he is loved more than all the people who visit his house, and his needs are considered before theirs. He also has to feel part of the caring team himself.

If only the mother in the fictitious story could have talked to her son at breakfast and explained, 'I've got a lady coming today who is very sad because she's lost her husband. I'm afraid she'll be bringing her little boy with her. Do you mind if he plays with some of your toys?. Perhaps I could help you put any special ones away in the high cupboard for safety.' Before the child went to school, they could have prayed as a family for the woman and her child. Children love being in secret league with you and God, and if they are treated like adults they are more likely to behave like adults. Prepared like that, the boy might well have felt like showing a bit of God's love himself and playing with the small child in the garden. He was fond of his own father, and would feel very sorry for someone else losing there's. Of course, the mother should have broken off her conversation and talked about the French trip the moment he came in from school. He probably only wanted two or three minutes of her complete attention, but he had a right to that. When the young man arrived, the child would have felt very much part of the team if his mother had called him quietly out of the sitting room, and explained her dilemma. 'I just can't talk to two people at once. Can you look after him for me? He hasn't got a family or even a home to live in, see if you can cheer him up.' Had she done that, she might well have found the two of them playing darts together later. A portable T.V. that could be used upstairs would have sent those two boys to bed feeling they were having a treat rather than a punishment.

I have discovered over the years that the presence of our children in the house has helped tense, frightened or miserable people to relax. When their needs are explained to the children (without, of course, breaking any confidences) the children respond in a wonderfully sensitive way.

Naomi and Nigel have a house group that meets in their house. One of its members used to be a fast talking con-man, until a terrible accident left him physically handicapped and emotionally shattered. He spends a lot of time in their home, and Naomi and Nigel have prayed about him with their children. One day he mentioned it was his birthday the following week, and the children decided he should have a secret birthday party. The oldest girl made him a cake and they all went shopping and spent their pocket money on all kinds of little presents which they wrapped with great care. As he sat opening up the biros, combs and sweets and blowing out his candles, the tears were constantly trickling down his face.

'No one had done anything like this for me for thirty two years,' he said.

'I think,' commented Naomi, 'the children enjoyed that birthday party more than any we had ever given for them.'

We also need to teach our children to care with us on a wider scale. They need to understand how many millions of children are dying for want of food, clothes and shelter. One family I know had bread, cheese and soup for their Sunday lunch for a month. Then the children were allowed to take the actual cash they saved on the joint and fancy pudding into the Tear Fund shop to help send relief to children less fortunate than themselves. Another family did much the same when they had fish fingers for their Christmas dinner. That was not much of a sacrifice – they preferred fish fingers as children often do!

In many Christian homes now you see the photo of a child pasted up on the kitchen wall. The children are proud to tell you 'that is our adopted brother'. Their parents are sponsoring a Third World child financially and by praying for him as a family, and sending him photos, letters and presents the children are being taught that individuals can be helped, even if the sufferings of the whole world are an overwhelming problem.

I think I learnt the importance of working as a team with our children a very few weeks after the events of the first chapter of this book. I was meeting the children from school and Justyn and his little friend Neil came out together.

'How's your Mum?' I asked him, knowing she had been in hospital for a few days after a slight heart attack.

'She's dead,' he replied in a matter-of-fact way. 'Daddy took me to see her yesterday, but they said we couldn't stop cos she'd just died.'

I had to turn away quickly, and I remember gazing at a clump of daisies on the bank while I fought a losing battle with my tears. I failed Neil in that moment, but Justyn stepped in and covered for me in childlike ignorance.

'Ask your Dad if you can come to tea,' he said, 'then we can play with my new football.' They both scampered off towards the man in Neil's waiting car.

He came to us frequently after school and at weekends after that. He did not want to relate to me. I could not take his mother's place – it was Justyn who did all the comforting. The worldless kind of comfort that comes from sharing the same T.V. programmes and getting together to make a model aeroplane.

Having said all this about teamwork, we must still recognise the fact that the presence of 'oddities' in our homes may frighten, revolt or embarrass our children at times. (When our teenage son brings home his new girlfriend for supper, that is not the night to invite the gentleman of the road as well!)

Like adults, children too have their vulnerable patches. Something causes them to lose their sense of security. Starting a new school, the birth of a baby brother, the strain of exams or an unsympathetic teacher. Often the first sign we have that something is wrong is their 'bad behaviour'. Frequently, when human beings are most in need of love they make themselves the least loveable! Yet the only cure for these insecure patches, is a double dose of our time and love. At certain times in our children's lives, we *must* remember that an Englishman's home *is* his castle, and lower the portcullis and pull up the drawbridge. If we give them all our attention when they demand it, they are less likely to demand it for long.

The older generation

What happens to our 'caring campaign' when we are faced with the responsibility of elderly or disabled parents? This problem can be a grinding conflict that faces many Christian families. Does charity begin at home?

Certainly it is easier to pay ten cheering visits to 'shut-ins' during a week, than it is to have our own bedridden or senile mother to live with us, and if we took on that responsibility we would have to give up that job which helps the family financially, and from which we derive so much fulfillment.

The world in this generation sees no conflict here. It is not fair, they say, to restrict our lives by caring physically for our old people when they could go into state run homes or hospitals. One hundred, or even fifty years ago, before the Welfare State this difficult decision was easier to make – there was no choice, and the older generation were cared for by their families and often died in dignity surrounded by their descendants.

The Bible has plenty to say about our responsibility to our parents, but the Bible was written in days when your widowed mother might well have been flung on to the street as destitute unless you provided a home for her.

There is an interesting section in Matthew 15:3–6 where Jesus seems to be saying that to honour our parents means to help them financially and He goes on to berate the Pharisees for teaching that if you are giving your money to God, you are excused the need for giving it to your parents. I wonder if the Lord would equate money here with time? If so, then I think He would not approve of us being His gloves to other people while neglecting our relatives.

The most direct biblical guidance we are given on this subject comes from 1 Timothy 5:3–4 and 8 (NIV): 'But if a widow has children or grandchildren, these should learn first of all to *put their religion into practice by caring for their own family* and so repaying their parents and grandparents for this is *pleasing to God* . . . If anyone does not provide for his relatives, and especially for his immediate family, he has denied the faith and is worse than an unbeliever.'

That is not a very popular idea in this generation. Does 'putting their religion into practice by *caring* for their own family' simply mean paying for a private nursing home or does it mean actually making sacrifices in order to be able to care in person? God is the God of the individual, and He guides His children along different paths. We have each of us to ask Him what He wants *us* to do. After all, we own nothing: our house, time, energy and resources are His, and if He wants them spent on granny, then that's what we must do.

However, it is important to realise that just because the Smithsons in our church have moved their granny in with them it does not necessarily mean God wants us to do the same. How, therefore, are we going to be sure we know what God is guiding us to do? Might we not just be hearing the voice of our own inner desires when we pray, and not God speaking at all? One thing I know we can always be sure of – if we ask Him He will not let us make a mistake. My mother was chronically ill in a nursing home, and Tony and I both felt we should convert our lounge into a bedroom and look after her ourselves. We prayed about it and then made preparations to move her. It was then that our baby son became terribly ill and was admitted to hospital. We put off mother's arrival until he was better, but it took fifteen long, hard months of round the clock nursing and endless hospital visits before he was well, by which time mother had improved vastly and was happily installed in a hotel! Five years later when she had a stroke we prayed again for guidance, and this time nothing stopped us from having her, and although I found looking after her the hardest thing I have ever had to do, I shall never regret the fact that she died holding my hand surrounded by the people she loved.

What was wrong on one occasion was right on another. God used drastic means to stop us, but stop us He did. If you are quite sure God has said no to you about the physical care of your relatives, then you must not feel guilty and condemned about your decision.

Obviously 'caring for our own family' as described in 1 Timothy 5:3 means ringing, writing and visiting frequently, supporting them psychologically as well as financially, and never allowing them to feel pushed out and forgotten, yet we must remember that it might not always be in the old person's best interests to be absorbed into a family.

We knew Frank and Janet quite well from church. They were a delightful young couple with two fat roly-poly babies. When Janet's father died her mother, who had a heart condition, seemed to collapse physically. Without actually stopping to seek God's will definitely, Frank and Janet brought her to live with them and sold her house in Manchester. Janet's mother had known the Lord for many years, but the shock of her husband's death seemed to sap all her self-confidence as well as her confidence in God. She became in her insecurity, incredibly demanding, and soon Frank and Janet's marriage began to suffer and the once happy home became a place of tension and arguments.

'It's all my fault,' sobbed Janet when she finally went one day to see our vicar. 'I feel resentful towards Mother for coming and spoiling everything, so I take it out on Frank and the children. Could you please pray that I will be able to cope with them all better?'

'First I would like to ask the Lord *how* He wants me to pray,' replied our very wise vicar, and after a silent prayer he said something to Janet that surprised her greatly.

'I think you are hindering your mother's recovery, both spiritually and physically. She is relying on you and not on the Lord. I believe she should be living on her own now, and trusting God for everything.'

The vicar was on the committee of a nearby sheltered housing unit and within six weeks he had found Janet's mother a tiny flat in this complex. A Warden was always on hand, and the flat was made very cosy with all the old lady's possessions.

'It seemed such a cruel thing to do,' Janet told me, six months later, 'turning her out like that, but honestly she has taken on a new lease of life. She visits the other old ladies, reads to two who are blind, and really seems like a different person. We enjoy her coming round here every Sunday, and it's no effort for me to pop in each morning to get her bits of shopping. I think we were probably smothering her before!'

If we are genuinely putting God first in our lives, and then our families, I am convinced that we can trust God to see they come to no harm by what He might lead us to do for other people.

11: *I'm too ill to be useful to God*

It is always a shattering experience even for a committed Christian, to discover that they have cancer.

'It all happened so quickly,' my friend Emma told me. 'I was in hospital having a complete masectomy before the full implications of the diagnosis really hit me. When I came home, I felt too weak and ill to do anything. Just living was exhausting, serving God in any way was out of the question, yet He used me all the same. We put a desperate advert in the Post Office window asking for someone to help with the housework for a while, and a girl called Sheila phoned up that same evening. I liked her immediately, and she soon had the house back under control. One day she came into the sitting room and plonked herself down by the sofa where I was having a rest and said, 'What's this "God thing" you've got going in this house?'

'What do you mean?' I asked.

'Well, all the Bibles by the beds and posters with texts on them, and you not seeming to panic even though you have got cancer?' I told her all about the Lord and discovered that she had been seeking Him ever since her brother became a Christian. By the time I was well enough to cope on my own, Sheila had joined our church. I laugh when I think about it. I never set out to help her, she came to help me!'

The secret of asking for help

It is much more blessed to give than to receive, and those of us who are giving ourselves to other people reap a massive reward, not only from the Lord, but also we experience the lovely warm feeling inside that comes from doing things for others. We must all remember however, that sometimes by dong things for people we can humiliate them. Giving feels good. Receiving is often very difficult. Sometimes the greatest thing we can do for someone is by being humble enough to receive their care so they can be blessed by being the giver.

I feel sure that is why Jesus asked the woman at the well in John 4 to give Him a drink. If she had thought He wanted to help her face up to all her sins and short-comings, she might have fled in fright. But she was disarmed by his obvious need. Jesus taught us a big lesson by His approach to that woman.

When Gill's marriage suddenly finished, she was so shocked she feared she was on the brink of a complete breakdown.

'My church friends were wonderful, but somehow I felt patronised by their kindness, knocked flat on my back by a wave of do-gooders. The real turning point for me came when an elderly church member who lived in my road arrived on my doorstep in tears. 'I feel terrible troubling you at a time like this,' she faltered, 'but I can't think who else to turn to – you're the only nurse we know.' Her very elderly husband had just had a slight stroke, and she did not want him to suffer the trauma of going into hospital, yet she felt she could not manage the blanket bathing on her own. I spent three months popping in and out of their house several times a day, and had the joy of seeing the old man regain much of his mobility. Of all the people in our church he certainly helped me the most. I know he prayed for me constantly when he couldn't sleep at night. And as I did the little practical things for him that made him comfortable he often used to tell me about all the wonderful things he had discovered about the Lord during his long life. But it was his helplessness that helped me. I had to be needed again, and looking after him restored my self-confidence. That old saint might easily have thought that he was useless to God in his weakness, but he certainly was not.'

We can crush people by helping them

When I made that list of hang-ups and inadequacies, so many of which were my own, I can see how God met me in them and healed me of so much. My self-confidence grew enormously over the years; but in my efforts to rid myself of shyness I probably over-did things, and like so many other shy people I over-compensated by becoming as bouncy as an over-grown puppy. Looking back now I think I must have been very irritating to the people I was trying to help. There was I, fit and happy with a lovely husband, six healthy children and a nice home. They must have felt I could not possibly understand their suffering. We need a lot of tact and gentle understanding, or we will crush the self-esteem right out of the people who need it most, simply by being too efficient! Certainly I think I went through a patch when I stopped being God's gloves and did things in my own strength.

Seeing things from the other side

Suddenly I lost all that strength and became disabled by a disease similar to Multiple Sclerosis. Being disabled made me feel, at first, totally useless to God. Suddenly people were doing practical things to help me and my family and I could do nothing for them in return, and it hurt. But gradually I have learnt that there are more ways of loving people than just scrubbing their floors or doing their shopping. There must be many Christians like me, who because of ill health or old age, cannot dash round and *do* practical things for people, but we have the huge advantage of always being *in* when anyone wants us. We have time to write letters and ring up other lonely people, and I believe that is a ministry in itself. Neither are we too busy to pray for people in need, and as John Wesley said, 'When I work Satan laughs, but when I pray he trembles.'

All human beings have a basic need to feel useful. Physical weakness does not need to rob us of the fulfillment of that need. Over the last four years, I have met many disabled Christians and I have realised that often *because* of their pain and frailty, they are more sensitive to the deepest needs of others than fit and healthy people could ever be.

When I first became ill, my eight year old son Duncan was bewildered by my sudden disappearance to hospital for several months. He became deeply disturbed emotionally. He would not allow anyone to penetrate the wall he built round himself to hide his anger and hurt. There were two hours between the time Duncan came out of school and Tony got home from work. Duncan refused to go to anyone's house or even to go home with the older children. I have already mentioned my disabled friend Andrea, who for years has struggled with a painful disease of the spine. Only she understood how Duncan was feeling, and even in her pain and weakness she had him to tea every day and let him play in her lovely garden until Tony came to fetch him. Of all the people in the village, she was about the least able to cope with a boisterous, aggressive boy. But it was to her that he turned because she understood his need to mend in privacy and beauty.

12: I'm on my own

'But we met at Bible College!' Rowan sat huddled at our kitchen table, her tears steaming up her thick glasses and blinding her. She and her husband Francis (a childless couple) had been leading members of our church and very much a focal point for the young people. Then Francis had fallen in love with a young and attractive girl who worked in his office. She was not a Christian, and for three tense years Francis and Rowan struggled to keep their marriage going. They went to Christian counsellors, conferences on marriage and read countless books, but in the end Francis packed his possessions and left to live with Mary. The strain of the previous three years, and then the sudden and final rejection hit Rowan hard in every corner of her being.

'This doesn't happen to Christians!' she said as she sat in our kitchen that day. But it does. For the next year Rowan, who had been such an outgoing member of our church, became an emotional cripple. She managed to keep her job as a nurse at the local hospital, but she spent all the rest of her time living on the circumference of three Christian families in our church. She just needed to be with people and to be constantly reassured.

Then one morning as she was reading her Bible, she felt the Lord say to her, 'Rowan, I want to use your house.' Like Sarah in the Bible (Gen. 18), Rowan laughed out loud: 'How could you want to use this place Lord? It's like a tip, I hate every minute I spend in it.'

It had been months since she had taken a duster to her home and piles of rubbish filled every available corner. The cottage was so small, it was impossible to swing a mouse, let alone a cat! She pushed some magazines off the armchair and sat looking round her lounge. A tile had come off the roof and the damp had seeped in pulling the wallpaper off the wall, and the windows were so dirty she could hardly tell if the sun was shining outside or not. Suddenly it dawned on her that she had been feeling increasingly lonely as she had spent time with happy, united couples and families. Their unity had accentuated her singleness, and however late she stayed out, she always had to come home in the end to a cold, ash-filled grate, unmade bed and her breakfast remains littering the kitchen.

'Perhaps if I did something about this place I might feel more like spending time here,' she thought, and that is just what she did. Her savings went on a new carpet, and some modern fitments for the kitchen, while the church rallied round with paint and wallpaper. Teams of us spent hilarious weekends decorating the little place. One man built her a new fireplace and mended the roof, another fixed the kitchen units in place and plumbed in the sink. Rowan made new curtains and re-covered her chairs and the transformation was hardly believable. One day as I sat by a roaring log fire in Rowan's new fireplace, I looked across the cosy little room and realised she looked happy for the first time in years.

'Now it's all ready for God to use,' she beamed, 'I wonder what He'll do with it.'

The next day Rowan went to buy some knitting wool at the local shop and found the girl behind the counter struggling to hold back her tears. It was her fortieth birthday and all she had ever wanted was to be married.

'Come round and have supper with me,' suggested Rowan. 'I get terribly lonely too, and it would be fun to cook for two again.' There was no room in Rowan's cottage for a table, but they sat by the fire balancing plates on their laps. It sounds a bit trite to say this, but it happens to be true! Peggy from the wool shop committed her life to God a few months later, and she was not the only person who warmed themselves physically and emotionally by Rowan's fire. God used her to help countless people, many of whom had gone through a tragedy similar to her own. In fact, Rowan allowed that experience to become one of her greatest assets in serving God.

I have to admit I often found myself envying Rowan her freedom to work for the Lord. I think that is what Paul was trying to say in 1 Corinthians 7:34 (MV). 'An unmarried woman or virgin is concerned about the Lord's affairs; Her aim is to be devoted to the Lord in both body and spirit. But a married woman is concerned about the affairs of this world – how she can please her husband.'

Sometimes Rowan would get a phone call just as she was coming in from work – someone needed her to go round and give them her time. They were desperate, they needed her right then. Often she ended up spending the night stretched out on their sofa. Out of her working hours she was a free agent, she could devote her time to people when they needed her. A wife, especially if she has children is far from free. She has to get a meal for her tribe, see that school uniforms are ready for the next day, pack up school lunches, hear the section from the reading book and supervise the recorder practice. Our husbands might feel lonely and rejected if we dashed off in the evening because someone down the road was feeling suicidal. Many bereaved or damaged people need undivided attention which married people just cannot give them.

People who are single, for whatever reason, are in the unique and privileged position of relative freedom which many of us envy greatly.

When the Rev. John Stott was asked to what he attributed his success in the ministry at All Souls in London, he replied, 'My singleness.'

13: I feel too depressed myself

When Margaret's husband died, her four children were
still young and their needs and demands left her little
time to think. However, once the youngest had left home
she began to suffer from odd bouts of depression. She
was so used to keeping her feelings buttoned up tightly
that she never told anyone how she was feeling; but for
days or even weeks together she felt her life was pointless, just a dreary waste of time.

'A Christian shouldn't feel like this,' she told herself
desperately, and when one day the young curate came
to see her, she was tempted to tell him just how she was
feeling. But before she could force herself to get started
he said, 'Margaret, I've come to ask for your help.'

'How could I possibly help anyone?', she thought
miserably as she poured him a cup of tea.

'I've just been to visit a woman in St. Jude's,' he
continued (St. Jude's was the local mental hospital). 'She
is in a very bad state indeed. Last week she took a
massive overdose of sleeping pills because she feels so
helpless since her husband has left her and her children
are grown up.'

'I know just how she feels,' thought Margaret, but she
merely passed the plate of biscuits.

'They are going to keep her in for a few weeks until
her condition stabilizes,' continued the curate. 'I just
couldn't seem to get through to her, and the sister said
she doesn't seem to have any visitors. You are about the
same age, and have the same kind of background, and

I was wondering if you could go and see her sometimes. I feel she is really longing to know God.'

This was just about the last thing that Margaret wanted. She did not wish to spend her time with someone who was depressed when she felt so low herself, but the curate looked so pathetic, she felt she just could not say no.

Next afternoon, armed with a bunch of flowers she set off for St. Judes. It was to be the first of many visits, and when Phoebe, the depressed woman, was discharged, Margaret spent many hours with her gently integrating her back into the outside world.

'Sometimes,' Margaret told me, 'I just had to hold her in my arms while she sobbed like a frightened child, but gradually she began to improve. It was quite a responsibility checking her pills and seeing she had enough food in the house. Once she disappeared for a whole day and I spent hours driving round in the car looking for her! Throughout I was very conscious of all the prayers and support I was getting from our church, and quite suddenly I discovered that I had not felt depressed once since I had begun to help her! Yet I think I was able to help her *because* I had been feeling so depressed. I think I had more sympathy and patience than other people might have had.

It was wonderful when Phoebe gave herself over to God completely. You could just see Him removing all her depression and putting His joy in its place. She began to go back to visit patients she had known at St. Judes. They introduced her to others, and soon she was a regular visitor, doing people's hair, shopping for them or just sitting and listening as I had listened to her.

They trust me because I've been one of them,' she says. 'Going back there gives my life a definite point and I have a reason for living now!" '

Depression is said to be the 'scourge' of this generation, and hardly any of us avoid going through this horrible experience in a greater or lesser degree at some time in our lives. In the context of this chapter we are naturally not discussing severe clinical depression, just the 'fog patches' that are so often caused by an imbalance of hormones, or our struggle to adjust to the changing circumstances of life. Redundancy, bereavement, retirement, the sudden isolation of being at home all day with small children or the feeling of no longer beeing needed when those same children leave home; the grief of a broken marriage or the effects of a serious illness – all these can cause depression. Just because we are Christians does not mean that these things do not affect us, and if Satan tells us anything different we can refer him to many people in the Bible who Suffered terrible depression, Elijah, Job, Jeremiah and David, to name but a few. Yet they all, like Margaret and Phoebe, illustrate the point that we can still be used by God even if we don't feel we can.

Trying to come to terms with disablement plummeted me into such a deep depression that some mornings I woke wondering why I had not been sensible enough to die in the night! Whenever I could, I would force myself to say through clenched teeth, 'Lord who do you want me to reach towards today?' I knew I had begun to light a candle in the darkness. Sometimes, even now my wheelchair feels like a mousetrap, but if I can just manage to ring someone up who I know is even more miserable than I am, then I begin to feel better.

Someone said to me once that she reckoned there were two ways of standing in a supermarket queue. One was to feel how tired you are, how your feet ache and wonder however much was this trollyload of goods going to cost? The other was to turn and smile at the old lady behind you and say, 'Lovely weather we're having aren't we?' People always love to talk about safe things such as the weather or the price of tea, and that old lady may not have talked to another human being all day, so her depression is lifted as well.

Many of us were damaged by events or relationships far back in our childhood. The Lord is able and willing to heal these scars, but He may not do so instantly. Just because we have hang-ups does not mean we cannot be used by God. In fact, I believe that people who have known or are experiencing His inward healing touch, are more able to bring others through the same experience.

It certainly seems to be true to say that depressed people are often cared for best by people who know from experience just how terrible they are feeling.

Danger!

Never tell anyone suffering from depression that they could be cured if they would only start reaching out and caring for other people. It may be true, but it is never wise. They must come to that realisation for themselves.

14: I have no gifts

It is all too easy to look round at our fellow Christians and feel how much more gifted they are to work for God than we are. Their sparkling personalities draw people like magnets. Their children are well behaved, their partners support them. They have been blessed with enough money to afford a house people enjoy visiting, and obviate the necessity to work which leaves them with more time to serve God.

Eric was the minister of a church in a very bleak area of a northern industrial town. Unemployment was rife among his congregation. One Sunday he felt led to say from his pulpit, 'We may not have much of this world's goods among us, but each of us has been given some special gift from God which He wants to use. Are you aware of yours? Are you using it?'

His remarks were met by a dead silence, and he knew that the point had hit home. Next morning, a very ordinary dumpy little widow came to his door. Eric had hardly even noticed her before because she was so insignificant, but she certainly seemed greatly distressed as he took her into the privacy of his study.

'I haven't been able to sleep all night,' she quavered. 'You said yesterday that we all had some gift that would be useful to God, and I've racked my brains, but I just can't think of anything I can do.'

'I want you to ask God every day for a week,' said Eric gently, 'that He will reveal your gift to you, and I'll come and visit you a week from today to hear what God has told you.'

The following Monday he had many visits to make and one couple's plight particularly distressed him. The wife had been disabled by multiple sclerosis for some years relying heavily on her husband, who had now become ill with emphysema. They were not churchgoers, but he had been asked to visit them by the District Health Visitor. He left them feeling deeply sad for their helpless condition, and made his way to the door of the woman he had promised to visit the previous week.

'Well?' he said, feeling his heart sink as he noticed her miserable expression.

'I've prayed all week like you told me to,' she said, 'but every time I pray, I just get this word *soup* coming into my mind. I don't think God's been speaking to me at all.'

'Oh yes He has,' beamed Eric, and proceeded to tell her about the couple he had just met.

'They have Meals-on-Wheels at midday,' he said, 'but what they really want is some nice hot nourishing home-made soup each evening – they live right in your street.'

'I used to love cooking,' she admitted, her eyes gleaming with excitement, 'but since I've been on my own there's been no point.'

Several years later Eric was preaching to his congregation once again on the subject of gifts, and as he looked around his church he saw two wheelchairs in which sat the couple he had visited so long before. They had both turned to Christ and were brought to the service each week by other church members. He also noted several other people who had been attracted to the Lord through the loving way in which this ordinary little woman had used her gift for cooking.

Gifts in odd wrappers

When Prissy lost her baby in a cot death, she certainly did not think of the experience as a gift from God. Now, four years later, although the grief is still there, she has been able to help and comfort many other families who are going through this same tragedy. When we hand our griefs to God in acceptance (and it sometimes takes years to be able to do this) we begin to see them as gifts. Just because we have gone through something ourselves makes us better able to help someone else in the same position. 2 Corinthians 1:4 (GNB) says, 'He helps us in all our troubles so that we are able to help others who have all kinds of troubles, using the same help that we ourselves have received from God.'

When our lives belong to God, all the experiences that we have can be turned by God into gifts to others.

15: What are our motives for serving God?

We have now steadily worked through the list I made of reasons why so many of us feel inadequate to move out and help people, and I hope we have discovered that many of them are actually *assets* to God. We have not, however, touched on what is probably our most common reason for doing nothing. We feel inadequate because we think *we* have to do something and we know we can't. We forget that no pair of empty gloves *ever* did anything useful. Once we have actually experienced God doing through us things we know we could never do in our strength, we shall never be the same again. Continuing for years to do the thing we know we can do quite adequately, never actually teaches us to trust God, and really after a while we become so expert we don't even need His help. It is when we launch out beyond our own ability that we are really being God's gloves. Once we have dared to do that, we feel more able to trust Him to take control the next time. Our 'God-confidence' has increased (see diagram).

Of course, we have to realise that there are some people who do not feel inadequate at all. In fact, they positively revel in the act of caring for people. Perhaps it was the way they were brought up or maybe they were just born with loving, outgoing natures. It is an embarrassing fact that many of these nice people are apparently quite godless, but live by much higher standards of honesty and loving kindness than a lot of the

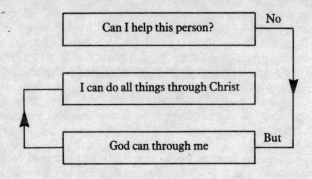

```
┌─────────────────────────────────┐  No
│      Can I help this person?    │──────┐
└─────────────────────────────────┘      │
                                         │
┌─────────────────────────────────┐      │
│  I can do all things through Christ │   │
└─────────────────────────────────┘      ▼
   ▲                                      
   │                                      
┌─────────────────────────────────┐  But
│       God can through me        │──────┘
└─────────────────────────────────┘
```

people who fill our church pews. But we will set that aside in the context of this book and take a look at the reason why we Christians serve others. Are we all like Mother Theresa of Calcutta who cares for people simply and solely for the love of God, or do we have many complex motives?

The need to be important

In any organisation such as a sports club, WI, Parent Teacher Associations or local political parties, there are always certain people who get on to the committee, organise the jumble sale or become the club president. Many justifiably feel they have been endowed with the ability to organise people and unless they exercised their gifts, nothing would ever get done. However, there are always others who take these positions of responsibility out of a deep desire to feel needed and 'important' within their community. The Christian equivalent often fulfil the same need by organising the various church departments.

Many women who give up responsible jobs to have a family, feel their talents and abilities are being under-used, and serving God can fill the void very nicely. People whose jobs or families do not absorb much of their time sometimes have huge reservoirs of energy dammed up within them, which have to find an outlet. God needs and uses people like that. At the same time, He is satisfying their very human need to have responsibility and standing within the community. It is not just the needs of the people we are caring for, that interest God. He is concerned about satisfying our needs at the same time!

Does it pay to advertise?

Jean was a truly remarkable woman and countless people in the district counted on her for practical support, but it was important to her that everyone else knew that. If you met her in the street she would gasp, 'Can't stop now! I'm rushed off my feet.' Then she would tell you at greath length and in tiny detail all that she was doing for numerous people. When she finally galloped away, you were left feeling small, useless and insignificant in comparison.

> The codfish lays a million eggs,
> The little hen but one,
> But the codfish does not cackle
> To tell us what she's done,
> So we despise the codfish,
> and the little hen we prize,
> Which really only goes to show,
> It pays to advertise.

It certainly did pay Jean to advertise, because looking back now over the years, I realise that Marilyn who also lived in the village, secretly did just as much for people but was so shy and quiet that no-one really noticed her in church – we were all too occupied thinking how wonderful Jean was. It has taken me all this time to discover just how much Marilyn did! If we want the approval of men we have to be like the little hen, but if it's God's approval we desire, we must be more like the codfish! When Jesus watched the Pharisees doing good deeds they had someone there to blow a trumpet, so everyone would see how wonderful they were being (Matt: 6 TLB). Jesus said, 'They will have their reward, the one they prize most highly, the praise and admiration of men.' But Jesus pointed out that by seeking that reward they would forfeit the far greater one that God would have given them one day, if they had kept their good deeds a secret.

Jesus did not condemn the Pharisees. They got the reward they wanted and the poor people were cared for. Jean also got her reward of admiration, and at the same time many people were helped by her.

The need to be needed

Some people, on the other hand, have no wish to 'blow their own trumpet', and be important in the eyes of the little world of their church, but they badly need to be important to the people for whom they care. I once knew a little girl who had lost both her parents. Any pocket money she received or coins she could steal went on buying sweets. She never ate them herself, but took them to school in order to 'buy' the love and friendship of other children. Many, like her grow into adults who still feel they cannot be loved for themselves, but only for what they can give or do. They have a great need for others to depend on them. God uses that need to produce some of the greatest carers of all, but He warns us in Matthew 5: 16 (AV) 'Let your light so shine before men that they may see your good works and *glorify your Father which is in heaven*'. Their good works glorify them in the eyes of the people they are looking after, and they do not always glorify God. In fact, in some cases they actually short circuit the blessing God wanted to give the person in need. We were falling into that trap with Yvonne, the girl who lived with us for more than a year and took an overdose every time life became rough. While she remained emotionally dependent on us, God could not get past us to help her. It was not until we stepped out of the way, that God could take first place in her life.

Amy Carmichael in her little book *If* writes, 'If I slip into the place that can be filled by Christ alone, making myself the first necessity to a soul, instead of leading it to fasten upon Him, then I know nothing of Calvary love'.

When we become over-confident in ourselves this can easily be our thought model:

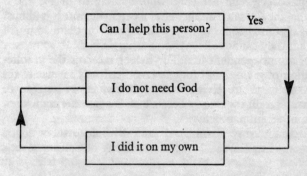

It is so very easy to feel that it is *our* common sense and good advice that is helping someone. *Our* company, the nourishment of *our* food, and the shelter of *our* homes that are building them up again as people in their own right. But we have to know, and they have to understand, that we are only channels of God's love. We cannot care for them for evermore, but God can and He will, if we help them to depend on Him and not on us.

111

The easiest way of doing this is simply to pray with them. When someone comes to us with their worries and problems, we often feel overwhelmingly sorry for them – and humanly speaking quite helpless. When we feel like that we should tell them so, and ask if they mind if we pray (they hardly ever do). I feel it is terribly important to pray with them wherever you happen to be. It only needs to be a short prayer, in everyday language. Of course, if you happen to be in a café or standing at the school gate, don't bow your head and shut your eyes – that would be desperately embarrassing. Praying in a natural way demonstrates that *we* are not the person who has helped them. We cannot heal wounds, but God can!

I know from personal experience that the 'loving care' of certain overenthusiastic people can completely swamp and overwhelm someone who is disabled or ill, and I imagine the same applies after a bereavement. It is almost as if some people want you to depend on them so much that they cannot allow you to struggle back to some sort of an independent life. The helper receives the gratification of giving, and forgets how hard it is for us always to be on the receiving end! Some invalids never recover from an illness simply because of the smothering love of another human being.

Again Amy Carmichael said, 'If I love to be loved more than I love . . . I know nothing of Calvary love.'

The need to gossip

There was a girl in a church to which we once belonged who was a marvellous listener. She had a real interest in people, but it was very hard to differentiate between that interest and an innate nosiness. Of course, she helped many people who felt far better when they had talked out all their worries, but it was not so helpful when she went round the church fellowship saying, 'Do pray for

112

so and so. You'll never believe this, but that husband of hers actually . . .'

Under the guise of a prayer topic she indulged in her enjoyment of a good gossip and hurt many people in that way. The Bible warns us in 1 Timothy 5: 13(GNB) not to be 'gossips and busybodies, talking of things (we) should not.' If we are ever going to help anyone we must learn to keep anything they tell us in sacred confidence.

The need for martyrdom

There are some people who are only happy when they are miserable. They simply love to be overworked martyrs. I would not have believed that was really true until I met Mrs. Robinson. Our vicar was a bachelor, and she kindly offered to do his laundry every week. You could never meet her after that without her working the conversation round to the unfortunate man's washing.

'I don't know why I ever took it on,' she would moan. 'All those surplices!' Everyone in the district soon knew about poor, overworked Mrs. Robinson, and the vicar himself was deeply embarrassed to discover what a burden he had laid on her. So he started taking his washing to his widowed mother. But when Mrs. Robinson discovered this, she was so offended she joined the Baptist church. The vicar had robbed her of the pleasure of being a martyr. Sometimes we feel that the things we do for God should be a duty and not a pleasure. In fact, if we enjoy ourselves we feel we cannot be doing God's will, yet we all know from our schooldays that we do best the things we enjoy doing. Why should God not want us to be happy in His service? Romans 12:8 (GNB) says, 'whoever shows kindness to others should do it cheerfully'!

The need to earn salvation

Perhaps down through the centuries, one of the strongest motives for doing 'good deeds' has been to earn salvation. This has probably been one of the greatest conflicts in the Christian church. Countless people think that the word 'Christian' means someone who is constantly trying to do good, kind things, and they have a mental picture of an old fashioned set of scales. All bad deeds are placed on one side and all the good ones on the other. If the good deeds outweigh the bad ones, we are allowed into Heaven.

The Bible teaches clearly that not one of us is worthy to reach Heaven however hard we try. It is only by accepting the death of Jesus in our place that our sins and mistakes can be covered. If our good deeds could balance out our bad ones, then His agonising death on the cross was a pointless waste.

The need to earn God's favour

Even when, as Christians, we have accepted all this we can still feel, (like the little girl and her sweets) that God can only love us for what we do for Him or give to Him. For some remarkable and mysterious reason, that simply is not true. God loves us just because we are *us*. More than anything else He longs for our company. Of course, He wants to work through us but our personal relationship with Him matters to Him far more.

This thrilling truth is perfectly illustrated in the story of Mary and Martha, the two sisters who lived in Bethany. When Jesus came to visit them, Mary sat at His feet and listened to every word that He said, while Martha thundered around the kitchen preparing the most lavish feast possible. She loved Jesus as Mary did, but she was only able to show it by *doing* things for Him, and Jesus gently pointed out that she was being too busy to develop her relationship with Him. I feel very drawn towards Martha because I have fallen into the same trap as she did. I have let myself become so involved with needy people, as well as coping with my large family, that I have found myself for long stretches of time, too busy to pray. 'To work is to pray' is not a motto for Christians. Unless we keep closely in touch with the source of love (God Himself) we are only handing out to people our own limited care.

John 11:5 is a huge comfort to me. It says, 'Now Jesus loved Martha . . .' He loves us too, and because He made us, He understands that we have a need to be noticed by others, and to be valued, needed and loved. I also believe He wants us to recognise these feelings that we have, so that we can prevent them from getting out of hand and spoiling our relationship with Him, or His relationship with other people. Constant introspection is never a good thing, and if we all sat round waiting for our motives to be pure, nothing would ever be done for God at all. Sometimes, however, it is a good thing to stop and take a hard look at ourselves. Why not find a pencil and paper and write down all the things you do for God, and then *why* you think you do them. Remember there may be a variety of reasons for each act of service.

Having made that list, by an act of faith hand it to God, asking Him to satisfy those needs, cover the failings and convict us of other wrong motives we have not yet recognised.

The acid test

There is one way of knowing for sure if the job we do is more important than the God for whom we do it. *How would we react if that job was taken away from us and given to another?*

Beena had no children and her husband was away a

good deal, but she certainly did not waste all the time she had on her hands. She was a born soul winner, but she also believed in making disciples and not just converts.

She had not been in the village a year before she had led three young mums to the Lord, and she started a weekly Bible study for them on a playgroup morning. She lent them tapes and books and took them to praise and healing meetings, where they could hear the best speakers in the country. In fact, she taught them all they knew about the Christian life and, being so much older than they were, she naturally looked upon them as daughters. After about two years of her constant care and nurture, they reached a 'spiritual adolescence'. One of them, who lived in the next village, felt she should start a little nurture group of her own. The other two felt they needed to join another much larger Bible study group where they could meet many more Christians. To put it bluntly, they all felt they had outgrown Beena and learnt as much as they could from her. When they gently explained this to her, they expected her to be pleased that they had matured enough to stand on their own feet with God, but poor Beena was devastated and deeply hurt. The rift between them has never been healed. Beena needed them more than they needed her. The spiritual power she had over them, had helped them through their 'infancy' but it had also gratified something within Beena that was not totally pleasing to God.

Of course, God accepts that we will serve Him for a variety of motives, but I think He wants us to try and keep on pushing two of them into the centre of this circle (see diagram).

I think the greatest lesson I ever learnt about serving God was taught to me by our friend Brother Thomas More. I have already told the story in a book called *Beyond Healing* (Hodder and Stoughton, 1986) – but I make no apology for telling it again! He was a Roman

116

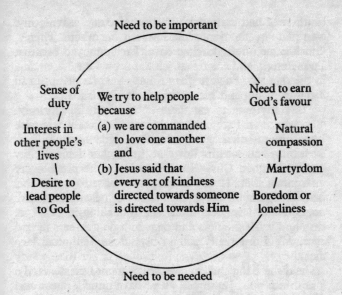

Need to be important

Sense of
duty
/
Interest in
other people's
lives
\
Desire to
lead people
to God

We try to help people
because
(a) we are commanded
to love one another
and
(b) Jesus said that
every act of kindness
directed towards someone
is directed towards Him

Need to earn
God's favour
\
Natural
compassion
|
Martyrdom
/
Boredom or
loneliness

Need to be needed

Catholic monk who lived in a small branch of his Order near our home. His job was to cook for the brothers – a task that he greatly enjoyed.

'I show my love for my brothers when I cook tasty food for them,' he would say. One day he told us about a dream he had had the previous week. With tears in his eyes he said, 'I dreamt the Lord Jesus Himself came into my kitchen and I wanted to cook the best meal possible for Him, but all I could find in the fridge was a piece of fish and some hard cheese. All the same I got to work and, as it often happens in dreams, in no time I was putting a plate before the Lord who sat at my kitchen table. I felt so proud of that meal, the fish was covered in a smooth cheese sauce, fluffy white potatoes and green peas garnished the dish and I longed to see my Lord enjoy it, but I woke before He started to eat.

A few days later I was dishing up the meal for my

brothers. I had carried it into the refectory, leaving my own plate in the oven while I served the others. Then a knock came on the kitchen door. I felt annoyed because I was hungry and anxious to get to my own meal. Outside in the rain stood a very dirty tramp, the rain dripped off his ancient hat and his tattered coat was sodden.

"Got anything to eat, Guv?" he asked. The rule of our order is that we must always give hospitality, but all I had was my own meal in the oven. Very reluctantly, I let him in and sat him down at the kitchen table.

"Smells good Guv," he said as I put the plate down in front of him. It was then that I realised that on the plate lay fish in cheese sauce, flanked by peas and mashed potatoes. As I watched him eagerly tucking in I had to turn and wash the pots and pans to hide the tears in my eyes. My Lord really *was* in my kitchen enjoying His meal.

-'and the King shall answer and say unto them, Verily I say unto you, Inasmuch as ye have done it unto one of the least of these my brethren, ye have done it unto me." (Matt. 25: 40 AV).'

16: How does our church look from the outside?

Have you ever stopped to consider how the church you attend looks to the other people in the district who never enter its doors? I don't mean the paintwork, or the neatness of the graveyard, but your reputation as a group of people who say they follow the teachings of Christ.

Phil and May lived in a village where there was a rather remarkable little Baptist church. They had never quite got round to going themselves on a Sunday morning, but when their first baby became very ill they felt instinctively they should ring the minister, simply because the church was known to care deeply about the problems of people who lived in the village, and also believed in prayer.

'My wife has to take the baby up to London tomorrow for all kinds of tests,' said the anxious young father. 'Would you pray for us?' Within minutes the minister was round at their house. He prayed for the baby and promised that the whole church would also pray for them all on Sunday. They not only did this, but Phil came home from work each day that week to find a meal ready cooked and wrapped in foil on his doorstep, and the day his wife and baby returned home, a big bunch of flowers awaited them. The couple were so deeply impressed that they started to attend the Baptist church regularly.

Spiritual obesity

Why are there not more churches like that one? We live in a time when the church of God has never had better opportunities to hear the word of God. While we are driving our cars or cooking meals we can listen to the finest preachers in the world simply by flicking the switch of a cassette player. The sale of Christian books is booming and a very high percentage of churchgoers now regularly attend midweek house groups for Bible teaching and discussion. We know in our head what Jesus taught and how He acted, but none of this teaching is any good until we get out there and start loving people in His name. Perhaps we are suffering from spiritual obesity – constantly taking in, but not burning up our calories by converting them into energy. James says, 'Do not deceive yourselves by just listening to His word; instead put it into practice' (1:22 GNB). And in Chapter 2:14–15 we read 'what good is it for someone to say that he has faith if his actions do not prove it? . . . Suppose there are brothers and sisters who need clothes and don't have enough to eat. What good is there in your saying to them, 'God bless you! Keep warm and eat well!' – if you don't give them the necessities of life?'

In South America there is a minister of a church who is a great Bible teacher. He attracts to his church hordes of hungry Christians and he spends hours preparing weekly spiritual feasts for them. One Sunday he preached on 'Love your neighbour'. The sermon went so well, and the people seemed to take it in so avidly that he planned out a series of sermons on the same subject. The next week as he walked up his pulpit steps with his neatly written notes in his hand, he felt the Lord say, 'I don't want you to give this sermon today. Ask the people how they got on loving their neighbours, and get them to testify to the way they have put last week's sermon into practice during the week.'

The minister was stunned.

'Lord,' he prayed inwardly, 'these people have come to hear me preach, they won't want to do the talking themselves.' But as the hymn came to its final cadence, he still felt the Lord was insisting on this strange course of action. 'Anyway,' he reasoned, 'they are such an attentive congregation there will be plenty of things they'll want to share'. But it seemed that his church was full of people who listened to the word and did nothing about it. For they all sat looking at him blankly when he asked how last week's sermon had affected them personally. In vain he looked towards his elders and deacons, his 'Big Givers' and the leaders of the different church organisations, but they were all silent. In the end a little man, who no one had even really noticed before, got up at the back and very nervously told how he had gone home after the previous Sunday sermon, and seen his neighbour – a man he scarcely knew – working on his car. He had spent the rest of the day helping that man take his engine to pieces, and by sundown it was working perfectly again.

'I was really ashamed because the time went by so quickly, I forgot to come back for evening church. I've felt bad about that all week but my neighbour is like my brother now, and our wives have gotten together, even the kids are friends.' After he had spoken several other insignificant members of the congregation spoke up too, and their testimony did more for that congregation, than a hundred sermons could have done.

John Wimber, whom I heard tell that story says, 'By our good works we will release the power of God into our communities.'

What does it feel like to visit our church?

I wonder how often our big thriving, loving churches are visited by people who are urgently seeking God, and yet none of us actually realised they were there. How would a complete outsider feel if they walked into our church? Who would meet them first? Probably one or two well-dressed, important looking men, who may appear to the newcomer as 'church bouncers', there to prevent the penetration of any undesirables! Sometimes, these men will find them a seat, but in many churches they would have to find their own, and that can be a nerve-racking experience. If they were early they might easily sit in someone's 'usual' place. (As a visitor to a strange church, I have on several dreadful occasions been turned out of someone's pet pew, and the embarrassment can be shattering!) If they were late, things could be even worse. Congregations universally occupy the back rows and hug the outside seats and will never move along towards the walls in order to leave seats free by the ailes.

Perhaps the actual service helps the stranger greatly, and he longs to talk to one of the happy looking people around him, but what happens at the end of the service? We all steam to the back of the church almost knocking the newcomer to the ground in our desperate attempt to catch so-and-so about the Wives Group, discover if Clare's had her baby, check the flower rota in case we're 'on' next week, and change our library book or borrowed tape. Of course, we all love meeting one another on Sundays. It is probably the loveliest part of the whole week, but usually by the time we've spoken to all our friends, any newcomers will have melted silently away.

One day I was at the hairdressers, when I heard an irate voice from the other side of the central mirror saying, 'I've been to St. Patrick's several times, but no one has talked to me yet.' I was mortified. We had been attending St. Patrick's for a year and although it was a very large church, we had always felt it was very friendly. I wanted to apologise, but by the time I was shorn, the owner of the voice had been put under the dryer and there is nothing so embarrassing as trying to talk to someone who has their head in a hairdryer.

'I'll look out for strangers next week,' I promised myself, and at the end of the service I noticed one at once.

'Hello,' I gushed as I bounced up to her, 'I don't think I've seen you here before. Is this your first visit?'

She looked me up and down as a weed killer might look at a nettle, and at last she said, 'I have attended this church every Sunday for the last sixty years as my parents did before me, and who,' she added witheringly, 'might you be?'

Whoops! Being a member of a very large church can have its draw-backs!

Danger!

Not everyone who walks into a church wants to be pounced on and welcomed with hearty enthusiasm. Some people prefer to 'feel' their way slowly into a church community. How do we know how a stranger wants us to react as we see them walking out of church? I think before we step up to them, we have to remember to switch on that current of God's love and deliberately let Him do the talking.

If we do manage to get into conversation with a newcomer, we must remember that there is a world of difference between saying, 'Come round for coffee one evening,' and 'come round for coffee *tomorrow* evening'.

Then everyone will know

The thing that attracted Phil and May to their local church, when they knew they needed help, was the church's corporate witness to the love and reality of God reaching out to people in the village. That is not the only way that outsiders can be impressed by looking at our church. Sometimes it is the way we care for one another *inside* the church that leaves the deepest impression.

Patricia had a bad back. In fact, it was because of her bad back that she found God. She was not a churchgoer, but she sent her two girls to Sunday school and one of them told her teacher that Patricia had been prescribed an intensive daily course of physiotherapy, but could not go for it because of the scanty country bus service. A group of people from the church decided to do something to help her. They organised a daily rota of car owners to take Patricia into hospital, ten miles away, but more importantly, they began to pray for her. They decided it would not be right to preach at her for twenty miles a day, but they did not need to. Because Patricia was so impressed by people who were willing to give up their time to her in this way, she began to go to church with her daughters. Long before the physio was complete, she had committed her whole life to God.

'When my husband walked out on me,' she said, 'I didn't think anyone would ever care about me again, but suddenly I've got God and a whole new family.'

Patricia lived right on the edge of a large council housing estate. Everyone else who lived on it had to pass her house which was surrounded by her hopelessly neglected garden.

'They all complain when the wind blows my weed seeds into their gardens,' sighed Patricia one day after church, 'but with my back I just can't do a thing out there, and since Reg left it's turned into a jungle.'

A number of people from our church felt very strongly that it was their responsibility to do something about Patricia's garden, so one fine spring Saturday hordes of us descended on it. People brought their own favourite forks, hedge clippers or mowers and all got work. The children helped too, and they thought it was better than Guy Fawkes when we started the huge bonfire of hedge clippings and last year's weeds.

124

We all had such fun that day, that all the people who passed us stopped and stared with open mouths. By nightfall, the garden was dug over ready to take everyone's surplus seedlings and vegetable plants.

Later in the week, two people were heard talking in the Post Office. 'I used to think that lot from the Free church were a bit odd,' said one, 'but when you see what they did to Patricia's garden, it makes you think there must be something in all this religion.'

'Yes,' answered the other person. 'She's changed so much just lately, she looks like a new woman. They all seem to have such fun together too, don't they?' she finished wistfully.

Jesus said, 'And now I give you a new commandment: love one another. As I have loved you, so you must love one another. If you have love for one another, *then everyone will know that you are my disciples*' (John 1: 34 – 35 GNB).

Not only was He giving us a new commandment, He was resting the entire credibility of the Kingdom of God on the relationships between Christians. I find that a deeply sobering thought.

17: Taking the roof off our church

We have been looking at our churches from a distance, trying to see them through the eyes of outsiders. Now let's actually dare to take the roof off our church and look down inside it to see if we are really behaving towards one another as God's gloves. Do we really care deeply for the people in the pews around us? Philippians 2:4 (TLB) says, 'Don't just think about your own affairs, but be interested in others too and in what they are doing,' and Galatians 6:2 (TLB) bids us 'Share each other's troubles and problems and so obey our Lord's command.' We all know these verses in our heads, but what really happens on a Sunday after the service?

'Hello, how are you?' we beam as we bounce up to our friends, but do we really *want* to know, or are we programmed to expect the standard answer, 'I'm fine, and you?' What would happen if that person suddenly began to tell us, right in the middle of the jolly hubbub, 'I think our marriage is falling apart,' or 'I get so lonely living by myself, sometimes I feel suicidal,' or 'My business is failing, I just can't pay the bills.' If they did dare to speak to us honestly like that instead of hiding behind a happy 'Christian face' what would we do? Probably we would make soothing noises while allowing our eyes to drift around the building behind them, looking for the people we would really rather be talking to. Or worse still, take a quick look at our watches to see if it's time the roast potatoes went in the oven.

Amy Carmichael says, 'If my interest in the work of

others is cool; if I think in terms of my own special works; if the burdens of others are not my burdens too, and their joys mine, then I know nothing of Calvary love.'

A church is not just a family, it's a body – the very body of Christ. If your knee hurts, you will use your hand to rub it, but the vast majority of Christians leave the knee to get on with it, or hope the vicar or minister will do something to help.

We go to church to worship God and to meet other Christians, but do we really only want to talk to the 'nice' ones? In almost every church there are the 'in' crowd. They speak the right jargon, go to all the meetings and never seem to suffer from any financial, health or marriage problems. Their children always behave well, and their infectious, jolly laughter carries right across the church. Naturally, they are all attracted to one another – they share so much in common. They are the perfect example of victorious Christian living, or are they? As they stand there in their happy little groups, do they realise they are turning their backs on members of the same body who are hurting inside or who have crushing problems that make them feel unworthy to be called Christians at all?

'Something has to be wrong,' someone said to me recently. 'Our church is full to bursting point with people who have personality disorders and chips on their shoulders. Surely the church is no place for them.' I couldn't help thinking of the words of Jesus in Luke 5: 31 (GNB): 'People who are well do not need a doctor, but only those who are sick.' Of course our churches are full of 'sick' people. We do not become Christians by being good or solving our own problems, but by admitting we cannot cope on our own, and turning to God in repentance and asking for His help. We do not become good instantly, (how I wish we did!) Nor do we always receive inner healing and freedom from problems all in one go. Sometimes it takes God a lifetime to re-make us, and even then there has never yet been a Christian who has gone off to Heaven absolutely perfect. We cannot be perfect until we get there. No, our churches are full of people who need the greatest doctor in the universe, God himself. But He wants to use us as His surgical gloves, as we help one another. So while we are all clustering round the church 'superstars', we are not really fulfilling this primary function.

James 2:2–4 (GNB) hardly seems to apply nowadays, or does it?

'Suppose a rich man wearing a gold ring and fine clothes comes to your meeting, and a poor man in ragged clothes also comes. If you show more respect to the well-dressed man and say to him, "Have this best seat here," but say to the poor man "Stand over there, or sit here on the floor by my feet," then you are guilty of creating distinctions among yourselves and making judgements based on evil motives.'

A doctor and his wife arrived in our church at just about the same time as Si. The couple were full of fun, and it was so easy to love them. Si, on the other hand, knew the inside of several of Her Majesty's Prisons intimately, and with a battered babyhood and two broken marriages he naturally had a huge need for love, time and company. Yet it was all too easy to invite the doctor and his family to a meal and chat to them outside church and many people did, but very few asked Si to come back for a Sunday lunch. Isn't that a modern example of James 2:2–4? Of course, caring for someone like Si, who has many complex problems, can be a very difficult job and not everyone is called or equipped by God to do it. Si desperately needed the members of the congregation to acknowledge him with a smile and greeting at the end of the service, and the few people who were able to open their hearts and homes to him needed the support and prayer backing of the rest of the church.

128

Yet sometimes when people like Si find the Lord, this is just what *does not* happen.

It might have been expected that the people in Matthew and Julia's church would have been thrilled when God gave them a remarkable love for 'down-and-outs', ex-convicts and junkies. They led many of them to the Lord and always seemed to have several people living with them while they sorted out their lives. However, far from receiving praise for their efforts, Matthew and Julia suffered some real persecution from their church.

'Fancy subjecting their children to influences like that!' people would say, or 'They are just too naive to realise they are being used.' At first, Matthew and Julia were terribly hurt. They longed for the church to support them, and enfold these new Christians in their universal love, but it was only ever one particular section of the church who did that, to whom God had given a similar care for these people.

'It was easy to feel angry with our fellow Christians,' said Matthew, 'and think they were only interested in the well-off respectable people. Then we realised, through the help of a great friend, that God is just as interested in professional people as He is in tramps and junkies. Some of our Christian brothers and sisters had been given a love for *professional* people, and were using their comfortable, well-furnished homes to draw these people into God's Kingdom. Julia and I would probably have felt very uncomfortable in their circles, just as they might have felt out of their depth with our friends. We were all of us going wrong by not recognising that we can't all help everyone. God gives us a 'feel' for the people He wants us to reach, but we should all be praying for each other and recognising that we are all working for the same goals.'

In large churches it is impossible to know everyone, as I discovered to my cost at St. Patrick's! This is the reason why house groups are so vital. The great majority of lively churches have now started small units of about a dozen people, each with a leader who can know and care for his charges much more effectively than the vicar or minister, and of course the people within the group can care for one another better as they become acquainted at a deeper level. As new people join the church they can be fed into existing house groups and will be able to identify more easily with a smaller group of people.

I believe that the spread of these house groups is helping to advance an exciting new era in our church life today. In Acts 2:44-46 we are told how the early church lived. They shared all they had, pooling their resources so that everyone had enough. They ate in one another's houses so that no-one was hungry or lonely. A lifestyle like that probably would not work in this country at this time, but within house groups many Christians are moving nearer to that model.

It was one of those wonderful warm spells in March when the sun shines through our dirty windows to reveal all the dust and grime of the winter. Someone said at our house group meeting that night, 'I suppose I'll really have to make a start on the spring cleaning.' There were five of us in the group who were still at home with small children, and while everyone else drank their coffee we groaned together about the horrors ahead.

'It seems such a waste being shut indoors cleaning, with a bored toddler grizzling round the bottom of the step ladder,' said someone.

'Why must we do it alone?' ventured someone else. 'Surely cleaning someone else's house is far more fun than doing your own. Why don't we all spend one day in each house, and get the job done quickly?'

The idea caught on wonderfully, and within the week all our houses were spotless – far cleaner than they would have been if we had worked on our own, because if you know that several of your friends are going to see all your messy corners you make certain they are tidy before they arrive!

Sometimes we sang spiritual songs from church as we worked or listened to teaching tapes when they could be heard above the roar of the vacuum cleaners. The children loved it, and left their mothers in peace while they enjoyed the fun of playing with someone else's toys. We all brought our own picnic lunch and the fun we had that week we shall remember for ever!

Carrying one another's burdens

We all have to face awkward and worrying situations sometimes, such as an interview or a hospital appointment. It is so lovely to be able to share that worry with a group of people who really care, and a real joy when several of them phone up during the week to say, 'How did it go, we were praying for you.'

One evening, a couple in our house group very hesitantly asked for prayer about a problem they were having with their daughter. They were deeply embarrassed because they thought that no-one would really understand what they were talking about – but they shared their concern all the same.

'We had *just* that problem with our girl last year,' said another couple. Not only was it a huge relief to know that their child was not some unique monster, but the couple who had already lived through that difficult stage, made a deliberate point of asking the child to their house frequently at weekends. Just having a few hours of peace on a Sunday relieved a great deal of tension in her parents' home.

In a small group like that, it seems the most natural thing in the world to share a lawnmower, electric drills or sewing machines, and many groups pool their Sunday lunches once a month and all squeeze into one house, or take a picnic into the country. The children have huge fun together and single people are spared the lonely hell that Sundays can often be. People were not really designed to live in huge communities, but in smaller family groups, where they feel safer and more relaxed. That is what house groups provide in the larger structure of the church.

Danger!

House groups have many advantages, but if they become a church within a church, and form a clique they can be very destructive indeed.

Another danger is smothering. We become so dependent on each other that when something goes wrong, we rush to ring our circle of close friends in the group and forget to pray!

We can also become so close to each other that we do not allow each other enough privacy. Many people who are hurting badly inside need to be given time and space in which to mend. It is all too easy to find a situation when that person is bombarded by a swarm of loving friends who all want to help and become involved, each with a different instant answer to the problem. Some times we just have to withdraw and surround that person with prayer from a distance.

Probably the greatest danger that can befall any really caring church or house group, is to turn in on to themselves and forget the lost world starving to death for want of love just outside the door.

The time wasters

If our enemy Satan cannot prevent us from caring for people then he employs another tactic. Tony and I encountered it very nearly in our 'caring drive'. A girl called Christa began coming to our church, and soon gravitated towards our family. We felt that was God saying to us 'Look after her,' and we were too inexperienced actually to stop and ask Him if He really did want that. Christa had many problems that stretched right back in to her childhood, and we spent hours with her letting her talk it all out. She found it difficult to relate to the other people who visited our house, some of whom were in great need, but we felt Christa needed us most and asked them to stay away for a while. Soon she had our undivided attention, which is just what she wanted. After weeks of listening, prayer and consultation with more experienced people, we felt she would never be happy until she had made some move back towards her family. This was her sticking point, and when we put it to her she simply could not take it and dropped us like hot potatoes, drifting on to another open home where she could start from the beginning and talk about her problems all over again. It was very humiliating for us to discover that she had been doing this in different churches all over town, and she had worked her way down to us! She did not appear to want to be helped at this stage because she loved the attention she gained through having problems – they were her only source of importance. When anyone really got near the core of her difficulties, she took fright and moved on. In this way, she had wasted the time of countless loving Christian people for some years. Time that could and should have been devoted to people who genuinely wanted to be helped.

When you experience anyone like Christa, you feel like slamming your front door shut on everyone and turning the T.V. back on, and that, of course, is just what Satan would like us to do. But we learn from our mistakes, and Christa taught us a lot. With experience, we all learn to spot people like her more quickly and we also lean harder on James 1:5 (GNB) 'But if any of you lacks wisdom, he should pray to God, who will give it to him.' Looking back over the years I wonder whether, even if we *had* stopped to ask God for guidance, He might not still have required us to become involved with Christa. Even if she did not want God to solve her problems, He still loved her dearly and who knows, one day someone might have helped her. God is a wonderful show-jumper. Even if we refuse a fence many times, He keeps gently bringing us back until one day, over we go.

Pure religion

If we are looking back to the early church as our pattern, we soon realise from passages such as 1 Timothy 5 that they assumed responsibility for those living alone without support. In fact, James 1: 27 (GNB) actually says what God the Father considers to be pure and genuine religion, it is this: 'to take care of orphans and widows in their suffering . . .' Of course, those were the days when many widows and orphans were destitute, but sometimes being without companionship seems almost as bad as being without financial support.

Recently I received a letter from a widow, who lost her husband less than a year ago. She says, 'I don't think Christians think of the appalling loneliness of widows. James gives strong advice about this, but the present day Christians ignore this verse and are all busy with meetings.'

Perhapss if one of the Christians from her church could have asked her round for supper and then taken her to the meeting with them, she might have felt less desolate. 'It is going to things on your own that is so awful,' she told me in another letter.

Mrs. Prentice fared better in her much smaller church. 'When Bert died,' she told me, 'there were so many forms to fill in and business things that he had always attended to, I just didn't know what to do. Then the treasurer of our church started popping in regularly and helped me sort them all out. After that, I stopped lying in bed all night worrying. He always had his tools in the back of the car, and never minded putting a new plug on the iron or mending the washer on the bath tap. When you've had a man in the house for forty years you feel so helpless about the little things.'

What about the orphans?

There are many children in care today, not just because they have no parents, but because their parents are too ill or unstable to look after them.

'Oh, but I could never foster children because I'd get so attached to them. I couldn't bear to give them back again.' I've heard countless people say that, and I believe it springs from a preoccupation with our own need of the child, instead of his deep need of us. A friend of mine has been a foster mother for years, and when she visited me recently she said, 'Bringing up your own children is hard enough, but looking after someone else's is one of the hardest jobs in the world, yet I believe that more Christian families should prayerfully consider it. You may only have a child in your home for six months, but during that time he will have lived with God because he has lived in your home. He will remember, not only what you told him about the love of God, but he will recall the peace and joy in your home.'

Christian families aren't perfect, but God lives in the middle of them, so children can't help but be impressed by His presence. Often when children have been abused and ill-treated themselves, they grow up to do exactly the same thing to their own children. They have no other example. Living with a Christian family can give them a glimpse of something better, which might be enough to break that circle of ignorance.

Another friend told me about her foster daughter, who

when she came to them seemed completely unable to relate to men or boys.

'One evening I went to bed after tea with flu,' she told me. 'The next morning Debbie came in to see me. I knew she wanted to say something but did not know how to make a start. I had built up a good relationship with her by then, and bit by bit I coaxed it out of her. She had sat all the previous evening cowering in the corner of the sofa, just waiting for my husband to abuse her sexually. Every man she had ever lived with before had always done so. She simply could not believe they could just sit and watch television together and nothing more. I prayed with her, asking God to take away that fear of men, and He really did. Now she is making relationships with men as easily as women.'

The modern 'widows'

Of course, these days we face a desperate problem that would never have occurred in the early church. One out of every three marriages break up. And even in our churches the figures are now reaching one in every five. The fact that this is so common in no way eases the suffering for the people involved. I have talked to many single parent Christian families, and over and over again people say, (even when they have been deserted by their partner) 'I feel the odd one out at church – a second-class citizen, frequently left out of social occasions, condemned for my mistakes and my particular problems are just not recognised.'

Molly was left with four small children and she felt deeply grateful when the church offered to pay their fees at the parish weekend.

'But as soon as I got there, I knew I'd made a mistake in going,' she said. 'Trying to cope single-handed with four tinies was a nightmare. The meals were the worst part. It was a cafeteria service, and when the gong sounded, most families split up, one parent would bag a table and settle the children while the other went to fetch the food. I had to manage on my own as I queued up with my tray, after the strain of finding five places together. The youngest children bawled because I had deserted them, and the two boys would play up because I was not there to keep them in order. No-one else seemed to realise how hard it was for me, and they just got annoyed by my children when they did not behave well. If only someone could just have helped me over those mealtimes, or perhaps have kept an eye on my boys while I got the little ones to bed, but they were all too busy enjoying their own weekend.'

One little boy told his Sunday school teacher how much he missed not having a father any more. 'But you have God as a father,' she reminded him. 'Yes,' he said, 'but God can't take me fishing.'

'I can just about cope myself, since Peter left me,' said another friend, whose husband had actually been the minister of a church. 'But I feel so desperately sorry for my son. He misses out on all the masculine things. Once the chain of his bike broke and there wasn't a dad there to mend it. I shall always be grateful to one man in our church who quite often rings up to say, "I'm taking my boys to watch football, would Jamie like to come too?" That means more to us than I could ever express.'

Singles

What about the people who never marry at all, how do their churches treat them?

'They tend to pity us,' snapped a very successful career woman I spoke to recently, 'and that we find intolerable! Their shallow assumptions and silly comments can hurt deeply. A man in my church said to me recently, "I can't think what the men are coming to, leaving a pretty girl like you on the shelf." I could have hit him. How did he know that I did not deliberately choose a stimulating career and more time to devote to the Lord?'

'Surely there are some Christians who would have liked to be married and feel very lonely,' I said. 'Do you think the church as a body is meeting their needs?'

'Probably not,' she admitted. 'I'm sorry to say it, but I think many married women hesitate to include a single woman in her family's social life, simply because she cannot trust her husband. Yet in this generation single Christians have probably never had such an urgent need for the company and love of their Christian brothers and sisters. You see the world is constantly telling us, that there is no necessity to be lonely if you are unmarried and that casual sexual relationships with members of the opposite sex, or even your own sex, are an enjoyable alternative. But the Bible we live by tells us that is sin. The conflicts that this permissiveness creates can be enormous, and if we do not find the love and acceptance within our churches, it is no wonder that so many people slide into the world.'

Not long ago, the minister of a very caring and lively church came to see us, and I asked him how his church was meeting these needs. He gave me a wry smile, and said, 'A few years back my wife and I discovered that many of our single members went alone to the Wimpy or local hotels for their Sunday lunch. Some even go home alone to bread and cheese. Since then, we have always entertained as many of these people to lunch and tea on Sunday as our house will hold, and I have frequently urged my congregation to do the same, but precious few seem to hear me. I think they feel they can only ask someone home for a cordon bleu meal. If only they would realise that bread and cheese in company often tastes a lot nicer than bread and cheese on your own! I'm afraid we have far too many lonely people right in the middle of our happy friendly church, and Sundays can be for them the gloomiest day of the week.'

It is all too easy to feel that 'playing the organ or Sunday school teaching is what I do for God.' Yet I believe that we are all responsible before God for the welfare and happiness of our Christian brothers and sisters.

18: Love your neighbour

Jim was late for the prayer meeting yet again! I could feel Mrs. Peters bristling in her seat, and I could almost hear her muttering, 'Why can't the younger generation be punctual?'

Poor Jim was just as shy as his wife Jane, whom I mentioned in the chapter on shyness, and it was not until his next door neighbour died, that we all realised why he had irritated so many people by clumping in late every Thursday evening. Each night after work, he had been rushing his supper in order to go in and help the old man undress and get upstairs to bed. He did the same in reverse every morning in order to prevent Mr. Park's worse fear from being realised. He never had to go 'into a home'.

'And all that time we never knew,' remarked Mrs. Peters softly.

There were lots of other things about Jim that we, at the church did not know, but his neighbours did. When the man down the road knocked on his door one Sunday afternoon asking to borrow some wall plugs, Jim not only lent them to him, but went and held the heavy shelf in place while his neighbour drilled the holes.

'He'd do anything for anyone, he would,' remarked the man next door. 'He never goes on about his religion, but that's what it's all about isn't it?'

I knew for sure that Jim and Jane were both far too shy to mention to anyone that they were Christians, but they did not need to. The people who lived round them could see they were different. The evangelist Gipsy

Smith once said, 'People nowadays don't read the Bible, they read us instead.' Once the people who live next door, in the flat above, or the bedsit down the passage see us going off in our best clothes every Sunday morning, they'll know we go to church, and even though we probably won't be aware of it, they will be watching us closely to see if there is anything in this 'religious lark'. So if we graze the wing of their new car, and fail to tell them, shatter their nerves by the volume of our praise tapes, or the shouting matches with our children, stink them out of their gardens by our bonfires, or wake them from their sleep by the hilarity of our departing house group, they will not be ecstatic when we ask them to our church guest services.

It must have been lovely living next door to the carpenter's shop in Nazareth, but Jesus actually lives now in us, so it should be just as good to live next door to you and me!

Soup and sandwiches

All day long Jane had been looking anxiously out of her window. Next door a huge removal van was disgorging furniture into old Mr. Park's house next door. The new neighbours were arriving. Jane's heart went out to the tired looking girl with the heavy baby on her hip and the grizzling toddler clinging to her jeans, but Jane just could not pluck up the courage to ask if she could help. It was a bitterly cold day, so finally she made herself fill a tray with mugs of soup, ham sandwiches and some of her homemade cakes and took it next door. The removal men beamed at her, but the girl with the baby did not look pleased. Jane could feel her thinking, 'nosy neighbour, interfering already'. The baby looked positively blue with cold, but when Jane nervously offered to take him into her warm sitting room, Gail said firmly they could manage, and Jane went home feeling she had done everything wrong. She did not see Gail at all the following week, and she certainly did not dare to call in. Then one night at about ten, she and Jim heard a frantic knocking on their door. It was Gail on their doorstep and an ambulance was parked in the road.

'I'm sorry to bother you,' she stammered, 'but I just don't know anyone else to turn to. My little boy has been taken very ill and I don't want to take the baby to hospital with us.'

'I'll sleep in there with him,' promised Jane. Gail scarcely came home for a week, her little boy was so ill, but the baby was perfectly happy with Jane, and her two little ones. Jane and Gail naturally became close friends, but it was not Jane, but her confident friend Sue who asked Gail to come to the Bible Discussion Group she ran in her home each Thursday morning.

'Jane never told me she went to anything like that,' said Gail, 'but if she's part of it, yes, I'd love to come.' It was Sue who actually helped Gail commit her life to Christ a few months later while sitting in her kitchen, but it had been Jane's practical love that had brought Gail to know Him.

It is not very easy to show that you love your neighbour if you don't know him, and harder still if he shows you clearly that he doesn't want to know you!

I've noticed while living in two country villages that people there seem to know, *and want to know* everything about you, almost before you know it yourself. But in towns things can be very different. People are either so absorbed in their own cosy happy little worlds and their circle of carefully chosen friends, that they do not need anyone else, or if life is going badly for them, they withdraw behind a barrier that shuts out the world. We Christians have our own fulfilling church life, and if our neighbours want to live their own lives we are tempted to feel 'why shouldn't they?' But Jesus actually loved those people so much He was willing to die for them.

He can see that they are going to a lost eternity, and His death on their behalf will be wasted. He can see the fear, worry and disillusionment behind their gleaming facade and He knows that He alone can help them. He has planned just where we live so that through us He can encounter them. But really we can't find the time, because there are so many things happening at church, if they really wanted God, (we argue) they would come along too.

Had that been the attitude of Jesus when He was on earth, He would have spent all His time in the temple, the synagogue or eating honey and locusts in the wilderness. Jesus did not wait for the people to come to Him. He went where the people were. He called James and John while they washed their fishing nets, and Peter when he was out in his boat. He went in to Matthew's Tax office and Zacchaeus's home, and met all their friends at the parties they gave. In other words, He went out and met people in their own territory.

'My minister's wife came to see me once, and gave me a terrible telling off,' said a friend of mine. 'I had felt very strongly that I ought to do something secular where I could meet people who were not Christians, so I had joined a Keep Fit class, but unfortunately, it clashed with our Tuesday church prayer meeting.

She wanted to know if I thought my body was more important than my soul. I still went to Keep Fit, but I felt guilty every time. Then one evening when we were changing, I got talking to Maureen. She had been brought up in a Christian home, but had not been to church since she married twenty years ago. She had joined the Keep Fit class simply because she was feeling so depressed, but she's fine since she's been coming along to church with me, and the minister's wife is actually talking to me again!'

Far too many Christians spend all their spare time with other Christians. Perhaps they feel it would be an unwise use of their time to join a secular Music Society, the W.I. or House Wives Register, a tennis or art club or to sign on for evening classes. After all, you can't very easily preach when you're playing squash or learning to 'throw a pot', but unknown to us, people who are God's gloves stand out in a crowd, and His love is more infectious than flu. We don't have to *do* or *say* anything, it's what we *are* that counts. People very quickly know if we really care about them. David Watson in his book *Discipleship* quotes this anonymous poem:

Not merely in the words you say,
Not only in your deeds confessed,
But in the most unconscious way
Is Christ expressed.

Is it a calm and peaceful smile? A holy light upon your brow?
Oh no! I felt His presence while
You laughed just now.

For me 'twas not the truth you taught,
To you so clear, to me so dim,
But when you came to me you brought
A sense of Him.

And from your eyes He beckons me,
And from your heart His love is shed,
till I lose sight of you, and see
The Christ instead.

Lonely in a goldfish bowl

Life was not going well for Hendy. She hated living in the middle of a large housing estate and se missed the job for which she had spent years training. Her two young children frequently drove her up her neatly painted walls and prevented her from taking much part in the life of her church.

'I'm going to have a nervous breakdown,' she thought one night. 'The next morning,' she told me, 'I was pushing the pram past all the other (what I secretly called) goldfish bowls, when it dawned on me that many of them contained young mums like me with small children. I wondered if they felt as lonely and cut off as I did. So I took my courage in both hands, and went round every house on the estate asking if any other housebound mums would be interested in a weekly 'company lunch'. The response was amazing. Soon every Thursday between fifteen and twenty of us sat round my lounge or garden getting to know each other while our kids played round our feet. Everyong brought something, such as a loaf of bread, hunk of cheese, fruit or cakes for the kids, and we piled it all on the table and took pot luck. It was enormous fun. Some of my Christian friends started coming, and although we never had a speaker or organised discussions, I think our attitude to God seemed to rub off on the others. One girl had a discount card for wholesalers, and we organised a shopping syndicate. By buying in bulk, we all had the benefit of lower prices. Then we started a system where we took it in turns for two of us to look after everyone else's kids one morning a week, so they all had a chance to get their hair done or windowshop on their own in peace. We also organised a baby-sitting circle. As we all grew closer together, those of us who were Christians soon found the others asking us about our faith, and even bringing their kids to Sunday school. The venture did not start out as a Christian outreach – just a way of saving me from a breakdown, but honestly, so many of those mums became Christians, we had to start a Bible study/prayer group on another morning for them all.

Then my husband realised that he did not know the husbands of the women I had got to know so well, so, with the help of the police, he organised a Neighbour-hood Watch scheme, and that really got all the men together marvellously. The following summer, we had a huge street barbecue right in the middle of the estate with every one pooling food, just like we did on a Thursday morning. It was a marvellous way of getting to know people, and ever since, God has just seemed to reach family after family.'

It is not always so easy

It is probably the easiest time of all to know our neigh-bours when we are all pushing prams or waiting together outside the school gate. But once we begin to go back to work it is much more difficult. That was just the problem I faced with Diana. The only contact I had with her was that she paid me to drive her teenage daughter to school with my children. I felt strangely burdened for Diana, and found myself praying often for her, as I racked my brains to think of a way I could make a contact with her.

'Do you think your mum and dad would come out for a meal with us one evening?' I asked her daughter in the car one day.

'Oh no!' she replied firmly. 'They are so tired when they get in from London they hate going out, and at weekends they do the house and garden and get the shopping in. They can't stand people.'

I felt a bit dashed, but I went on praying. One evening our house group were meeting in our home, and I felt I should share my concern for Diana with them, and we prayed for her. I felt annoyed when the doorbell rang, but reluctantly I left the room full of praying people only to find Diana's husband on the doorstep. His pinstriped suit was crumpled and his face was white.

'Diana's had an accident,' he said, 'her leg and ankle are broken in five places. She'll be in hospital for a few days, but then they are sending her home in plaster. I don't quite know what to do,' he added suddenly looking very near to tears. 'They say she won't be able to walk a step for at least three months. We haven't made any friends round here, and I wondered if you knew of anyone who would be willing to pop in during the day sometimes and see if she's alright.'

I could have hugged the man. I felt sorry God had answered our prayers in such an unpleasant way for Diana, but this was the chance we had been waiting for! Again we prayed for Diana and then made our plans. For three months, one of us went in every day and cooked lunch for Diana. She needed help with the loo and odd bits of shopping, but it was a far from easy job. She knew she needed help, but she was fiercely independent and hated receiving it! I did not understand then why she felt like that, but I certainly do now I am disabled!

Towards the end of her 'prison sentence', I went in one day and found to my amazement that she was reading a brand new Bible.

'I asked my husband to get this for me,' she said, looking very embarrassed. 'I wanted to find out what makes you Christians tick.' After that we could hardly get through the door before her barrage of questions began. She was a highly intelligent woman, a member of Mensa and she was not going to get embroiled in anything she did not fully understand. When she was back to work again, I feared that she might lose touch with us all. But no, she and her husband started coming to our church and even joined the house group. Now they are both Christians.

The neighbour who needs us most

For the last twenty years I have been haunted by a pair of sunken eyes gazing up at me from a wrinkled, emaciated face.

'Don't ever grow old Jen, don't ever grow old.' The memory of that quavering old voice can still reduce me to tears. I was twenty-three, engaged to be married, fulfilled in my teaching job and about as happy as I thought it was possible to be. She must have recognised the contrast between us as she looked up at me from her crumpled pillow. I often popped in on this elderly neighbour because she too had been a teacher in her time, and loved to hear the latest doings of my inevitably naughty boys.

But how could I possibly have known then what it felt like to be old? Since I have been disabled, I have begun to realise a little more. The pain of knowing you are a burden on those around you and the feeling that the world is racing on, excited and busy without you can be worse than physical pain. Yet I still don't know what it feels like to be alone, the last of your family and circle of friends, degraded by bodily functions that no longer work properly, and forgotten by people who once respected you. Each new day holding a burden of worry as finances dwindle and you fear the fall or stroke that could sentence you for ever to a geriatric ward. One old man told me the other day, that he sometimes makes himself jump at the sound of his own voice as he accidentally talks to himself.

Recently, a question was asked in the leader's meeting of a very thriving church; 'Why is it that the support, visiting and care of the older members of our church is all carried out by other old people, most of whom are almost as needy as the people they are visiting?'

I suppose none of us can ever really know how it feels to be old until it is almost too late to help other people.

My council Home Help, whose job it is to care for many senior citizens, said to me the other day, 'If every family visited and felt responsible for just one old person, it would prevent so many of them getting so lonely and forgotten they just give up and die.'

Perhaps we should all be praying for someone to adopt!

Something we can all do

Some of the ideas in this chapter have made us feel tired before we start, or we know perfectly well they would never work in our district. But there is one form of caring – the greatest of all – that we could all be practising. That is regularly and systematically praying for our neighbours. Hudson Taylor once said, 'Men can be moved by God through prayer alone.' We probably don't know all our neighbours by name, but as we walk to the shops we can lift the occupants of each house to the Lord as we pass it. One friend of mine draws himself a little street plan, and he 'lets his fingers do the walking' as he prays. It is very easy to tut with annoyance as we look out of the window and see the badly behaved children from over the road playing football near our greenhouse, or hear the deafening roar of the motorbike belonging to the boy with the spiked orange hair. But if each time we became aware of these people we shot up an arrow prayer for them, our attitude would change even if nothing in them appeared to be different. How do we know that the jogger who pounds past our window at 5.30 each morning is not being influenced by God through our sleepy prayers? He will probably never know why he started searching for God – and we will not know until eternity that our prayers were answered. Prayer is the secret way of loving our neighbour.

19: God's gloves at work

'It was coffee-break one morning when I really reached a record "low",' said Beth. 'The job was so boring and repetitive I suddenly banged down my mug and said out loud, (but to no-one in particular) "I just can't think why I'm here". A very shy and quiet girl who I have been working with for the last six years looked up and said, "You're here because you are the only one who can tell us about God". I was stunned. In all the years I've been at work I can never remember telling anyone about God. "What do you mean?" I asked curiously. "Well," she replied awkwardly, "you often talk about the things that happen at your church, and it all sounds such fun, and you're different from other people aren't you".'

It can be so easy to go off to work feeling 'this is just my secular job', so we take our 'Christian' hat off when we clock into work and pick it up again on the way home. Yet working with us may be the only opportunity that some people ever have to come into contact with God, living in a human being.

It would, of course, be a disaster if we preached piously at everyone who came into our office, yet we must always remember that we shall influence every single person we encounter during the course of a working day. The person pushing the tea trolley or 'sir' himself will either be 'lifted' by us, or their spirits will go down a notch. We all transmit vibes that convey gloom and bad temper, or we can give off a definite aura of peace and joy. We can make people either feel liked and accepted, or despised and rather a nuisance to us.

My father always said, 'If your face wants to smile – let it. If it doesn't want to – make it'. Of course we don't always feel happy. Christians are human beings and we live with the same sorrows, stresses and fluctuating hormones that everyone else contends with. However, it remains a fact that when we relax our face muscles and smile, it is actually helping our own inner conflicts as well as demonstrating the joy that Jesus promised to give us. The people we work with cannot see God's face, so ours has to do! Perhaps we should build the habit of putting into God's hand every morning *all* the people we will contact that day and ask Him to bless *each one*, not just the difficult client or the autocratic nursing officer, but also the chance meeting we shall hardly remember by the evening.

Negative or positive

Kevin had worked for three years at one branch of a chain of shoe shops. When he was offered a transfer to their shop in Manchester, he went to say 'goodbye' to the minister of the church he had been attending.

'I feel I've failed somehow,' he said sadly. 'I've tried to witness at work, but no one has ever responded.'

'Do they all know you're a Christian?' asked the minister.

'Oh yes,' replied Kevin, 'I don't smoke or swear, and they know better than to tell dirty jokes when I'm about. They see me going into the local church for my quiet time each lunch hour when they're on their way down to the pub, and I wouldn't dream of going to the staff party.'

'Those are all rather negative things,' smiled the minister. 'Have you been able to show them the love of God in practical ways?'

'Well no,' replied Kevin, rather impatiently, 'you see

I don't think they like me very much, and I haven't really got anything in common with any of them anyway.'

'Well you have, you know,' said the minister, 'you're a human being! Have you managed to get them talking about themselves? Do you notice when they look off-colour? Would they confide in you if they had a row with their wife or broke up with their girlfriend?'

'Well no,' protested Kevin, 'I don't really know them.'

'I'm not surprised,' continued the minister grimly. 'Why didn't you have your quiet time before work, so you could go to the pub at lunchtime with them and get to know them as people?'

'But I'm a teetotaller,' said Kevin deeply shocked.

'Lots of Christians are,' countered the minister, 'but you could drink orange juice. Look, you've got a chance to start all over again in a new job. Why not turn yourself inside out and start showing positive love for people instead of a negative attitude?'

About three months later the minister had a letter from Kevin which he will treasure for a long time.

'I took your advice to heart,' it said, 'and I've tried to see myself as God's visible representative in this shop. It's been a bit hard because I don't hit it off with the manager to say the very least! Colossians 3: 23 (GNB) helped me so much: 'Whatever you do, work at it with all your heart, as though you were working for the Lord and not for men'. I hated the thought of working for the manager, but when I realised it was God I was really working for, it eased things greatly.

'One of the lady assistants asked me the other day why I always look so happy, and the funniest thing happened when I went into the pub at lunch one day. I ordered a lemon and lime, and the colleague standing next to me suddenly said, 'I'm so glad you're on the waggon too. I'm not supposed to have alcohol with the drugs I'm taking, but I always feel such a fool drinking a soft drink on my own. I usually give in and have a pint of bitter'.

I asked him why he was on these drugs, and he told me all about the depression he's been having since his wife left him. I'm going to help him decorate his flat at the weekend, we've become really good friends.'

They expect higher standards

We would probably be amazed if we know just how closely people at work watch us. Ruth was a staff nurse in a busy district hospital, and one day she was sharing a coffee break in the canteen with one of the other staff nurses from her ward.

She had heard a sermon on witnessing at her church the previous Sunday, and so she felt she ought to maneouvre the conversation round so she could talk about her faith.

'If you are really a practicing Christian,' demanded the other staff nurse, 'how come I have to cover for you so often when you go sick just because it suits you?'

'Everyone does that,' retorted Ruth sharply.

'Of course,' replied the other girl, 'but I thought you'd live by higher standards than the rest of us.'

Most people do expect us to be different, so we are really letting the Lord down when we behave as other people do. What kind of impression do we give when we:

Are last to arrive and first to leave

Grumble about the boss behind his back

Fail to pay for private phone calls

Charge for expenses we did not incur or fiddle our travel claim

Allow our juniors to carry the can for our mistakes

Become bitter when we are passed over for promotion

React angrily when we are made redundant

Allow personality clashes to ruin the atmosphere for everyone

Complain when people 'put upon' us
Are unhelpful or impatient when others ask for information
Are sarcastic or tyrannical with the people under us
Gossip unkindly when people go out of the room.
Tell white lies or get our secretary to tell them for us
Allow our bad moods to affect the lives of everyone round us
Are so inefficient we make extra work for everyone else
Do something dishonest because the boss tells us to do it

That is quite a list! No one is going to be perfect on all those points every day of their working lives. What a relief it is to know that none of us will ever be worthy to be God's gloves. All we can hope to do is to try and keep on thinking 'How would Jesus behave if He had my job?'

'It's all very well,' grumbled a friend of mine the other day, 'but most of the Christian leaders and Christian 'superstars' who shape our thought and give us all our teaching just don't know what it's like working in the real world.' He may be right, but it is interesting that Jesus spent approximately eighteen years in a secular job and only three in 'full time spiritual work'. He does know what we're up against, and He is right there inside us facing it with us.

What if we are not popular?

'I just don't know what I'm going to do about Ernie,' Mary flung her considerable bulk down onto our protesting sofa and sighed. She was in her first job, filling shelves at the local supermarket and Ernie was the manager. 'However hard I try, he's always on at me,' complained Mary. 'I think it's because he's found out I'm religious.' Poor Mary was learning early in her career that not everyone will like us, and when we are living for God we can actually constitute a threat to other people. They did not all like our Master and He warned us that things would be no different for us. Mary was part of our house group and that evening we were studying Matthew 5: 43 – 47. When we reached verse 44, 'love your enemies, and pray for those who persecute you' (GNB), she sat bolt upright, and the sofa groaned again.

'That's what I'll have to do to Ernie,' she said, 'pray for him.'

Later, when everyone had gone, Tony was rather pensive as we washed up the coffee mugs together. I knew something had been worrying him for several months, so at last I asked him right out what it was.

'Well, Mary's not the only one who has to contend with an Ernie,' he admitted. 'I've got Jack Dench,' It seemed that ever since Tony had joined the staff of the comprehensive school, Jack had gone out of his way to be unpleasant. 'It's systematic malice,' said Tony. 'The other day I was following him out of the staff room and he knew I was behind him, yet he deliberately slammed the door shut in my face. I nearly broke my nose. He makes sarcastic comments about me to pupils and constantly tries to make trouble with our head of department. He keeps sneering about Christians in front of me, so I know it is a spiritual rather than a personal thing, but he's making my life a misery.'

'What are you going to do about it?' I demanded, full of wifely indignation.

'Well truthfully,' he admitted, 'the last week or two I felt I was really going to hit him. He's asking for it, but dear old Mary really helped me this evening.'

So we both started to pray for Jack as well as Ernie. Because he believed that love is an active word and not just an emotional feeling, Tony deliberately looked out for small acts of kindness that he could perform for Jack.

'I got his coffee for him this morning,' he reported at the house group meeting, 'and when I knew he was doing a particular topic with one of his classes I lent him two books I had on the subject, and last Friday he was in a hurry to get home, but found his car had a puncture, so I helped him change the wheel.' Mary seemed to have done so well with Ernie, that he had asked her out for an evening at the wrestling!

We have a very special picture hanging on our wall, signed by Jack Dench. He gave it to Tony when he left that school four years later. They had become very close friends. In fact, after eighteen years we still exchange Christmas cards. Jack has not become a Christian yet as far as we know, but we pray for him every time we drive through Westerham where he was born.

'If someone has done you wrong, do not repay him with a wrong. Try to do what everyone considers to be good . . . If your enemy is hungry, feed him; if he is thirsty, give him a drink; for by doing this you will make him burn with shame. Do not let evil defeat you; instead, conquer evil with good' (Rom. 12: 17, 20–21 GNB).

20: I was sick and you visited me

It makes my hair stand on end sometimes when I look back at myself, as a healthy, fit woman trying to visit the sick. My tactlessness must have caused so much irritation. Now after four years of illness and frequent, lengthy hospitalisation, I have learnt so many lessons; but I have to laugh when I realise I am not really well enough now to put them into practice!

Twenty-five easy ways to make the sick feel even worse.

1. Speak as loudly as you can, ill people are always deaf.
2. If you've been ill yourself tell them all about it in detail, they'll be fascinated.
3. Keep looking at your watch and shuffle restlessly in your chair. It's good for them to know how many other much iller people you have to visit today.
4. If the person you are visiting is being fed by a drip, has a stomach complaint or diabetes, chocolates will make a perfect present.
5. Why not lend them some really deep theological books to pass the time.
6. Never ask them 'what shall I bring next time I come?' They might only want something dull like a nail file or envelopes.
7. It won't matter if you go out of ward visiting times, the sister won't be cross with *you*.
8. The more visitors a person has at once the better, so

157

never bother to ring relatives before you go to the hospital, it won't matter at all if you clash with them.

9. If you can possibly manage to be there at the same time as the patient's husband or wife, that is excellent. They won't want to be alone together.

10. Do give them news of their family. If their wife is looking tired or their children are behaving badly, they ought to know. If their garden is looking like a jungle or their pipes have burst, it will worry them; but they must know the truth.

11. Ill people love to have the Bible read aloud to them, so find some good long chapters, preferably from obscure parts of the Old Testament.

12. Always have one special verse you give to all sick people. Don't bother to ask the Lord which verse He wants them to have.

13. When you pray with the patient, do it as loudly as possible. It will be a good witness to the people in the other beds, so don't forget to include all their most personal needs.

14. Don't be inhibited in prayer – stand up and lift your arms in praise. If the patient looks embarrassed, it's only because he is such an immature Christian.

15. Tell them how nice it must be for them to have nothing to do all day but pray and study the Bible, especially if they are in a lot of pain.

16. Tell them you've seen this coming for months. They've brought the illness on themselves by over-working. Feeling guilty will do them a power of good.

17. Do try and minister to them on a deep level, remember you are much more spiritual than they are.

18. You probably know exactly why the patient is ill, they are their own worst enemy. Share your opinion with as many people from church as possible.

19. Don't go and visit anyone who is terminally ill, that could be embarrassing.

20. When someone is ill at home, you can stay much

longer because you won't be limited by silly visiting restrictions. If the patient looks tired, don't worry, after all, you've travelled a long way, and they ought to be glad of a good visit.

21. Don't, whatever you do, look round the house while you are there in case you see plants that need watering or some ironing or dusting. Remember you are there to talk, not to work.

22. Try and keep looking as serious as possible, after all illness is no laughing matter.

23. If you pay a state visit to inspect a new baby, be careful not to take any notice of the older children in the family. It's the baby that matters, they must learn that jealousy is wicked.

24. It is better not to visit people who are nervously or mentally ill; but if you do come across someone who is depressed, tell them how easily they could shake it off if they stopped thinking so much about themselves.

25. While they are convalescing, keep warning them to be careful. Discover what they feel they can do, and then stop them. The aim is to destroy self-confidence at all costs.

I must hurriedly point out that not all these things have been said and done to me, nor, thank God, did I do all that to other people; but sometimes 'negative brainstorming' can serve to emphasise a point more deeply than a list of soothing advice.

21: Bereavement

We are embarrassed by death

Victorians never mentioned sex, but nowadays death is
the taboo subject. This world worships youth, health
and fitness; and because medicine has made such massive
advances, we feel doctors ought to be able to cure everything. This philosophy is not confined to the secular
world. It has seeped into the lives of people with strong
religious beliefs and the passionate interest with which
many Christians view the healing ministry, can easily
give the impression that death is the worst thing that
can ever happen. Yet surely as Christians we believe that
this life is only a fragment of our eternal existence and
death is the gateway to a better life? So why are we so
embarrassed by death?

'A few days after John died I went into church to
collect some odds and ends he had left there,' said Bettie,
who is the widow of a greatly loved clergyman. 'Two
of our church members were arranging the flowers for
Sunday, but when they saw me, they hurried out of the
side door rather than have to speak to me. The same
kind of thing also happened when I went round the
village. It was being ignored by other Christians that
hurt the most.'

Perhaps it is not so much embarrassment that we feel,
but a reluctance to intrude into someone's private grief.
Yet all the many bereaved people to whom I talked
before writing this chapter, all agreed that any action or
contact on our part is infinitely better than none. What

ever we do, we *must do something*. It is not enough to feel that the doctor or vicar are trained to cope with 'that kind of thing' and hope that the bereaved will 'get over it' quickly and cause us as little embarrassment as possible.

'I was alright once someone had made that first contact with me,' said Eve as she recalled the loss of her first baby. 'I felt too embarrassed to go up and speak to *them*, but if they came to me, and even just said "hello" I felt I could be comfortable with them again.'

Everyone is different

So we have established that bereaved people do not want us to ignore them, but that still leaves us with a massive problem. What kind of contact and help do they want?

Everyone that I talked to seemed to mention something different that they had found helpful, and the stories they told of remarks and actions that definitely did *not* comfort them, were horrific! Grief is such an individual thing, that there does not seem any standard formula for those of us who long to help.

Usually people in shock don't really know themselves what they need, and our previous knowledge of their character will probably not assist us either, because people under stress often do not 'run true to type'. Physical contact, such as a quick hug on the doorstep or a squeeze of the hand may suddenly become important even to the shyest of people, who could surprise themselves by needing a house full of companionship, while more gregarious people long for solitude. Many highly capable people suddenly find they need help with the housework or cooking, while the actual routine of daily life helps others to keep their sense of security.

Many long to talk endlessly about the person who has died, going over and over the details of their last hours. This might embarrass us dreadfully and we may feel they should be distracted and helped to take an interest in other things. Yet bereaved people can see this as an apparent lack of interest and be deeply hurt.

As we face this huge divergence of need, how can we *know* how to act and react? Once again, we have to switch on that current of God's love, and by an act of faith trust Him to show us what to say and do.

We must do our best to be unshockable. Some people may behave in their grief in a manner that seems to us rather odd. When Michelle's husband was killed, she had her hair tinted and bought a new dress for the funeral.

'Anyone would think she was going to a wedding!' remarked her shocked neighbours, but for Michelle the only way she could face the ghastly day was to know that she looked as nice as possible.

Don't be surprised by bitterness and depression

When Job lost his ten children and all that he possessed, he behaved very well at first, but as the months went by he began to feel depressed and angry with God, and said so without inhibition. His nausiating friends were deeply shocked and blamed him for being the cause of all his own misery. How like those friends we can often be. We do not expect other Christians to behave like that and feel they should be a joyful witness to the whole neighbourhood. His friends plied poor Job with good advice until by Chapter 21 he shouts in desperation, 'Listen to what I am saying, that is all the comfort I ask from you, give me a chance to speak' (Job 21:1–2 GNB). God gave him the time he needed to express all his bitter feelings, and he finally talked his way back to faith. Are we prepared to do that? Marie did it for her friend Rosie.

'I could have accepted the death of my little girl more easily,' said Rosie, 'if I had not believed in a God who could have cured her leukemia and yet He did not. For

162

a long time I really blamed Him, but I actually missed God desperately and almost felt doubly bereaved. I felt I could not show how I was feeling to my church friends. Only Marie understood, and she was prepared to help me on a long term basis. I used to pop into her house every morning when I dropped the other kids at school. She just used to sit and listen while I talked about my angry feelings, then she would pray out loud for all the everyday things that were worrying me, even though I could not pray myself for months. She encouraged me to keep a diary of how I felt each day, trying to make me write down anything positive that helped me, such as a verse from the Bible or a walk in the country. I treasure that book now, even though I used to think writing it all down was a waste of time.'

The inevitable guilt

Another thing that may surprise us is the feeling of guilt that is so often a reaction to bereavement. We can be irritated by this apparently unnecessary feeling, if we do not realise that the grieving person's thoughts can go round like a never ending video.

'Why did I nag him to move the wardrobe?' or 'I should have insisted the doctor did more for his pain.' Even after months of careful nursing, the guilt reaction makes them feel they should and could have done even more.

'It was at the funeral that I first began to feel that way,' confessed Ann. 'So many people talked about how wonderfully brave Rod had been as he battled with cancer for so many months, and what an example he was, but no one said, "and you did a marvellous job looking after him". Suddenly I thought perhaps the frustration I often felt had showed more than I thought it had, and I began to lie awake worrying that Rod might have sensed my feelings too. If one or two people had

163

told me they thought I'd been as brave as Rod and given me a bit of praise, that guilt might have been counteracted.'

Anger

Anger is another reaction that we may not expect. Some people cannot allow themselves to be angry with God – or with themselves through guilt, so they vent their angry feelings on their comforters, and I assure you that some of the most placid people can be really fierce!

It is vital that we develop the gift of speaking to anyone in a state of crisis from a position of looking up at them in praise and encouragement, rather than down on them as an instructor.

Some do's and don'ts are universal

Everyone who I talked to felt they really needed help for a far longer period than most people were prepared to give it.

'My Christian friends were completely wonderful when my wife died,' said Reg, 'the only trouble was that at first I felt completely numb, "asleep inside". It was not until weeks later that I realised just what had really happened and I felt myself collapsing. By then, people had stopped arriving with puddings and cakes, the flowers had died and the postman no longer delivered comforting letters. Everyone had drifted back into their own lives, feeling no doubt, that I was managing well, but that was when the loneliness really set in.'

It is easy to feel impatient with people who do not seem to be 'getting over it', as quickly as we feel they ought. 'You should be getting out more – find a job' we say bracingly, without allowing the person enough time to mend emotionally.

'Christians often feel they must offer spiritual counselling and good advice in hushed, unnatural voices,' said a widow who had known the Lord for many years. 'What they said to me was true, but it was often said too soon. "This is the beginning of a new life," they might say, while I wanted the old one back again. Or "Why don't you move out of this big house now?" Sensible, yes, but I was too exhausted after months of nursing Peter to face the upheaval of a move just then.'

Some common nightmares

Many people seem to fear going out at first. Seeing people scuttling into side streets to avoid meeting you can be very unnerving. Yet they all agreed that it did them good to go out even if they did not at first feel like doing so. Those of us on the outside of the grief should take the initiative here and not be deterred by a refusal at the first time of asking. Going out for lunch or a drive in the car can break up a dreary day. Shopping can cause sudden unexpected attacks of panic, but going with someone else makes all the difference.

Nearly everyone seemed to dread going into church alone and sitting by themselves. The offer of a lift and company in the pew is greatly appreciated.

During the first few days, the phone seems to be more of an enemy to most people than a friend, but later it comes into its own. There are certain patches in the day that are harder to live through than others – such as the time when a husband or child would have returned home, or early in the morning when the future seems to look uglier than usual. If we can discover these vulnerable times and ring them, we can fill the blank.

Because we have been bereaved ourselves, we may long to say, 'I know just how you feel,' yet that statement seldom seems to help, simply because everyone grieves differently. I heard of one well meaning man who called at the house of a young woman who had lost her mother the day before. He stayed for two hours and recounted in detail the stories of how he had been bereaved *three times*!

'My own grief was so enormous,' she told me, 'I just could not cope with anyone else's.' Eve was not comforted either when the vicar said, 'Don't cry dear, my daughter lost *two* babies.' Losing one was bad enough!

People can often be very tactless when they choose verses from the Bible to give or send. I am sure God would guide us over the choice if we took the trouble to ask Him and so prevent the kind of lasting hurt that Kathleen suffered.

'It is thirty years since I lost my tiny son,' she said, 'but I still feel blind rage when I remember a worthy Christian man giving me this verse on a card "The Lord gave and the Lord taketh away, blessed be the name of the Lord". (Job 1: 21 AV) Surely,' she commented, 'that is the finest response we can make to bereavement, but we all come to accept the death of a loved one at different times. It took me well over a year before I could repeat that verse with conviction. Having it forced on me too soon was disastrous.'

Rebuilding self-confidence

After Corin lost her beloved handicapped son, she travelled through a very desolate wilderness.

'But I can remember the day I began to come back to life,' she said. 'A neighbour rang me saying she had flu and asked if I could meet her children from school. I had been on the receiving end of so much kindness for so long, my self-confidence had gone. To be needed again began the mending process.' Sometimes the best way we can help someone is to ask them to help us!

What about people who don't believe in heaven?

It is usually most difficult of all to talk or write to bereaved people who do not appear to have any Christian faith. Yet strangely they often love to know they are being prayed for and eagerly listen to our beliefs about a life after death. Naturally, we must never preach at them, but neither should we miss the opportunity if they seem responsive, of giving them hope for the future at a time when they are probably most likely to accept it.

Death is not the only cause of bereavement

Sometimes it can seem easier to cope with losing someone we love through death than it is to experience their deliberate rejection and desertion. As Christians, we believe we shall be reunited in Heaven, and that knowledge can be one of the greatest comforts in bereavement. But for the parent whose adolescent has left home and vanished, or the third person in a love triangle, there can be no such comfort. They need all the attention, care, understanding and love that we have discussed in this chapter, and perhaps something even more important – acceptance.

Sympathy letters

We may not live near enough to our bereaved friend to pop in with a cake or a bunch of flowers, and after praying we may feel that a personal encounter is not the most helpful thing for them anyway. So we are faced with writing the most difficult letters of all. Everything I have learnt about bereavement, convinces me that there is no such thing as a standard letter. But here are just a few tips from people who have been on the receiving end.

1. Letters of sympathy must be simple and sincere. Sermons, stiff formality, spiritual jargon and long flowery sentences are *out*.

2. We need to focus on the person who has died, mentioning them by name and recalling something they did that helped us, or some quality that we admired. If we describe a happy memory from the past it will help the dead person to live on in our perception of them.

3. In the early stages of grief, people don't want to be distracted from thinking about the person they have lost, so don't be tempted to mention your holiday or the new car.

4. Exaggerated eulogies only irritate the family who loved someone simply because they were so delightfully ordinary. Insincerity will be easy to spot and it will hurt.

5. Cards can help if we really don't know what to say, but they should always be personalised by a short message. Beware of trite little printed rhymes.

6. Bible bookshops now sell verses printed out on little cards. *Just choose one*. A widowed friend of mine opened an envelope and out fell seven – she felt they had been mass produced! Remember her, and pray you find the right one. It is never helpful just to send a Bible reference, write the verse out for them. People in shock or who are ill simply cannot rummage through their Bibles to find a particular verse.

7. Etiquette books say sympathy letters should be handwritten, but if you can't write clearly – type them. They won't have the concentration to labour over a spider's handiwork.

8. Remember the guilt reaction they may be feeling and praise them for the things they did for the dead person.

9. It is important to write not just to the widow or widower, but also to the children or elderly parents. They often feel left out.

10. We need to write briefly at first, but remember to write in more detail after a few weeks and keep writing

as the months go by. Nothing we can say in a letter will be able to remove the pain, but a loving message may soften it for a while.

22: Helping in a crisis

Our mouths go dry and suddenly we may feel cold all over as we hear the news. Perhaps the husband of a friend has had a car crash and is on a life-support machine, the mother of a family has been given a month to live because of cancer of the throat, the teenage son of a neighbour has been arrested for drug pushing or has suffered a nervous break-down.

When we are trying to be God's gloves, we must remember that we are not the same as other people. We have the huge advantage of being controlled by someone who actually knows just what contact the family need most even if, humanly speaking, we do not. But before we start to act on His behalf, we need to *feel* as He is feeling. He is not just sitting comfortably in Heaven looking on in a detached kind of way. He is hurting with them, minding for them, longing to help them when they need Him most. If they do not know God very well they may not realise that, and we are the only channel through which He can convey His loving concern. Often when life is at its blackest, it is then that people move closer to God than ever before. Perhaps that is because He *feels* closer to them, and often the best way we can pray for people in crisis is to ask that they will have a deep sense of His presence. But let's be perfectly honest. How often have we said or written to someone, 'I'm really praying for you', and yet we never actually spare a few of our precious minutes to kneel down and do just that. Of course, we can pray as we dash round, but if we could really see God standing there, and if we *really* believed He is who we say He is, we would give the activity of praying a far higher priority in our lives.

There are probably two main ways we can help people in a crisis.

1. By staying away from them. We may not want to be left out of a good drama, but some people are exhausted by being surrounded by far too many people to whom they have to keep being grateful. Perhaps some flowers of just a card saying that we are praying, is the most loving way we can act.

2. By being there. When Jesus was facing the greatest crisis in His life in the Garden of Gethsemene, He said to his three closest friends 'The sorrow in my heart is so great that it almost crushes me. Stay here and keep watch with me'. When they failed Him by falling asleep He said, 'How is it that you three were not able to keep watch with me even for one hour?' (Matt. 26:38, 40).

Everything seemed to have gone wrong for Maggie, a Christian friend of mine whose faith I have always admired. Her son failed his A levels and went on to drugs, her daughter of fifteen became anorexic and dwindled down to six stone, and then her husband walked out on her after twenty years of marriage. The morning I heard the news, I went straight round.

'Kick me out if you'd rather have peace, but if there's anything I can do, I'm here.' I said. She did not actually want me to do or say anything, she just wanted my company. We sat in her lounge drinking a chain of coffees and demolishing a box of tissues. To 'weep with those that weep' was the only comfort I could give her.

Almost as soon as I got home, the phone rang and I heard the voice of an earnest, but very tactless Christian friend.

'I saw your car outside Maggie's all day,' she said. 'I

do hope you were able to counsel her and help her sort out some of the mess she's got herself into.' I was so angry I did not trust myself to speak. There are some situations that cannot just be patched up by a few soothing platitudes, and there are no neat answers to some suffering this side of eternity. So I put the receiver down, and hoped she'd think it was a fault on the line!

The telephone – friend or foe?

In this generation, we have the ability to keep people company without actually having to be with them – we can use the phone. I'm actually a bit frightened of it, and feel sure I'll ring at just the *wrong* moment. Perhaps they have just staggered in from the hospital and all they want is a quiet cup of tea or they've had ten calls already that evening and giving the same depressing news over and over again has lowered their spirits to zero. Yet my friend Barbara told me the only thing that kept her going while nursing her mother through the last weeks of cancer, was the phone, and the love that poured through the receiver. All the same, I don't think we should ever touch the phone before we have asked the Lord to help us choose the right time.

Help to share the load

Of course, not everyone is like Maggie, who wanted inactive support. If you are trudging back and forth to a hospital while trying at the same time to run a home, hold down a job or cope with children, there could be few things more *unhelpful* than someone who just sits in your lounge while the everyday jobs pile up around you. It is never any good saying vaguely, 'give me a ring if there's anything I can do to help'. In a crisis people are usually far too mindblown even to know what help they need, and few of us like asking for help anyway. It is

172

far better to decide after prayer just what assistance you could manage to give and then do it without fuss. The other day I rang a friend who is in the middle of a family upheaval (after praying earnestly that I would choose a good time!) She is a hugely independent woman, but she was nearly crying with relief as she told me,

'Valerie has just turned up, and says she's going to hoover right through the bungalow. Her husband's out cutting my lawn, and Cynthia spirited away the washing before half past eight this morning!'

Children

Some adults seem to think that children can only hear remarks that are actually made to them directly. Many parents realise that children in the midst of a crisis can be deeply upset by overhearing unwise comments and statements that are not properly explained to them. So when some well-meaning friend asks all kinds of questions and demands all the tragic details while the children are in earshot, their lack of tact can cause untold harm. Walls have ears, and so do children!

Very often even in the most loving homes, the children's needs can be overlooked in the pressure of a crisis, and sometimes we can help the whole family most by giving the children our time. If we sit and read a story, take them out to the park or down to the sea for a picnic, not only will it relieve their parents, but it is a way of claiming the promise given in Matthew 10: 42(TLB). 'And if as my representatives, you give even a cup of cold water to a little child, you will surely be rewarded.' This verse shows us how amazingly precious little children are to God.

Danger!

We always try instictively to comfort a family with a member who is physically ill or has been involved in an accident. However, the people who tend to get neglected are those whose relatives are suffering from the more socially unacceptable mental illnesses, such as depression. Bell had always been known as a 'carer' in her church, but then her husband's business folded and he went into a severe depression. No-one rang, wrote a card or dropped in to visit.

'I felt completely alone,' she told me some years later. 'It would have been such a different situation if he'd had pneumonia or a car accident.' Some illnesses are just not respectable, but that does not make them any easier to cope with for the people involved.

23: Caring for the carers

Gwen sat in the peaceful garden of her country home gazing absently at the distant rolling Downs. The letter that lay on her lap made her feel uneasy. It was from her friend Zaida, who with her husband Dick, had opened their spacious suburban home to a number of 'damaged' people and formed an extended family. 'One is coming off heroin,' wrote Zaida 'and two have drink problems. We've got one battered wife and one who hasn't been out of prison long.'

'Oh dear,' sighed Gwen as the bees hummed round her quiet garden. 'I know I could never have anyone to live with me like that, I need my privacy too much.' Suddenly the beauty that surrounded her felt like a selfish indulgence.

As she re-read the letter, she sensed that Zaida and Dick were very tired. 'They ought to get away on their own with their kids for regular weekends,' she thought, 'but I suppose finances would make that impossible.' It was then that she realised she had two bedrooms free while her daughters were away at university. 'So that's when I started, what I call "my spoiling weekends" ' she told me. 'They come down every six weeks, leaving their home in the hands of a couple from their church, and I just pamper them. They have breakfast in bed, and go out together when they like, while my younger kids entertain theirs. We try to get them to treat our home like a hotel and not feel they have to be polite to us and talk all the time. Entertaining on a short term basis like that is something I *can* do, and I feel I am enabling Zaida and Dick to go on with the work I so much admire them for doing.'

Gwen is not the only friend of mine who uses her home for the Lord in this way. One retired, but very active couple furnished their spare room specially with visitors in mind.

'We put a kettle and teatray up there,' they said, 'our portable T.V., electric blankets in the beds, and we keep a tin of biscuits and a basket of fruit frequently replenished. Many of our guests are clergy or missionaries, but often we have someone who is coming to terms with bereavement or redundancy. We don't feel we are here to counsel them, but just to wait on them as we would on the Master Himself.'

Helping people to go on caring

We think nowadays a good deal about the plight of the young mother imprisoned at home with small children, yet it is staggering to realise that a greater number of people now look after elderly or disabled relatives in their homes and are much more trapped than they would be by children. It is usually quite a simple thing to find a babysitter, especially if you belong to a Babysitting Circle, but not so easy to find 'a Grannysitter.' You can strap a toddler into a puschair and take him out with you, but I soon discovered when I had my mother to live with us that if I left her to dash to the shops, she forgot when I said I'd be home and went out in her petticoat to look for me, or tried to make a cup of coffee and scalded herself. I shall never forget the kindness of a friend who sometimes came in during an afternoon and sat with mother so I could get out into the fresh air for a walk, but how many other 'carers' are as lucky? It is not always a help to them to call in and ask for a shopping list, they need the stimulus of getting out to the shops themselves, while we stay in their homes.

Holidays for the carers are vital and several other friends of mine regularly have a handicapped child or an elderly person to stay in their homes so their relatives can get away for a rest.

Perhaps we are not called on by God to care full time for another human being, but if we are aware of the intense problems of people who are, there are probably many ways that we can share their heavy load.

24: Loving by post

There was no-one at the nursing home who knew who he was, or that before his stroke he had not only been the minister of a thriving church, but also a well-known Bible Convention speaker. Now he was just the frail old man in Room 4, who had so few visitors.

Then one day a letter came. He peered through his glasses at the signature, but it was unknown to him.

'Please forgive me for writing,' the letter began. 'I have wanted to for a long time, but I have had great difficulty in obtaining your address. Twenty-five years ago I was brought to your church and the sermon you preached changed my life. I had many personal problems, but after a few visits to your home they were ironed out. I am now the minister of a large Baptist church myself, but humanly speaking it is to you that I owe my faith and my ministry.'

The pleasure that letter gave to the lonely old man was quite out of all proportion to the price of the stamp or the half hour of time that it had cost the writer.

Letters are one of the most tangible ways that we can show love, yet so many of us feel we are no good at correspondence. But our letters do not have to be works of English literature. One widow told me that she had received several hundred letters after her husband had died, but the one that helped her most was simply a page ripped from a notebook with, 'Just heard the news, simply shattered, but do know we are praying for you', scrawled across it. It is terrible to feel forgotten and out of touch with the world, but a pretty card and a short message can give enormous pleasure knowing that someone cared enough to send it. Cards also come in to their own in times of crisis such as the morning a student starts exams, the day someone begins a new job, goes into hospital for tests or appears in court to fight for the custody of their children. On a morning like that, no one wants to read an epistle, a card says it all.

There are, of course, some people who actually like writing letters, and this can be a wonderful way to care for people when we are less physically active through illness or old age. Many people also find both writing and receiving letters much less strain than a personal encounter. Certain people, when they live through a period of trauma find it more helpful to communicate their deepest feelings to someone who lives a long way away than talking to someone amongst their circle of friends. Sometimes when I have written one of those awkward sympathy letters, I have found myself entering a deep relationship with the person I'm writing to, despite the distance between us. I learnt the importance of this way of loving people through my Aunt Geraldine. When I was grinding through the depression that followed my disablement I just could not relate to any of my loving friends. I actually hid if I heard them ring the doorbell. Humanly speaking, the one thing that sustained me through those black months was receiving letters from my Aunt. She lived in a remote part of Scotland and bashed away on her ancient typewriter several times a week, telling me all the funny little details that filled her days in the country. She never sent me verses or sermonettes, but simply told me about something the Lord had shown her that had greatly helped and blessed her. She did not convey the impression that I ought to be helped by them too – yet so often I was! I could read her letters at my own pace, and I did not have to make an immediate response. Soon, however, I began to enjoy replying, picking out of my life with the children, things I felt would make her laugh as well. There is nothing like searching for something funny in every situation for helping to cure depression, and soon I was feeling better. She taught me the great importance of commenting. Not just writing your news, but discussing the points made by the other person, and so creating a conversation.

The other day I received a letter from someone who said "Before you began to write to me regularly, I was so lonely, I used to write letters to myself sometimes! It is not a bad idea to mark our new diary in January to remind ourselves to write to certain people monthly or bimonthly. Out of sight can certainly be out of mind, unless we make a serious commitment.

Another good idea, is to keep a large stock of cards that contain no specific message, then you can send one out instantly when you hear of someone in need.

How to write to someone who is dying

One of the loveliest parts of a holiday is our anticipation of it. Nowadays, because of our embarrassment about death we can easily rob people of their joy in looking forward to Heaven. Last year I lost my very dear friend Rowan, whom I mentioned in the chapter 'I'm on my own'. As her death from cancer drew near, she reminded me of a bride joyously preparing for her wedding day. 'The things of earth grew strangely dim, in the light of His glory and grace'. I took my cue from her and in my letters I shared her excitement about Heaven and all the joys she was so soon to taste. When I went to see her a few days before she died she said, 'Thank you for mentioning death; when people do, it builds my faith so wonderfully.'

Not everyone, however, is like Rowan and many people who have an equally strong faith in Heaven, simply could not cope with their illness unless they continued to believe they were soon going to be well.

I also wrote regularly to another friend who died last year, and this was how he felt. In my letters, I kept to subjects such as T.V. programmes I knew he enjoyed, the holiday he was planning when he 'got better' and I frequently asked his advice about gardening. He needed to feel part of the real world still. When caring for people through writing, as in every other way, flexibility is vital.

The sudden urge

Sometimes for no accountable reason, we get someone on to our minds and we just cannot stop thinking about them. I think this happens when God wants us to pray for them, but it could also mean that we should write them a letter.

Nurse Peel was only on duty in my ward for one morning when they were short staffed, and she was assigned to bath me. When you have to be lowered into the tub by a mini-crane, you feel such a fool that it is a good coping strategy to get the nurse talking about herself. It worked a treat with Nurse Peel, and I soon discovered that she had a father who was a clergyman even though she had married a man who was an atheist.

'I've got a friend who is a Christian,' she told me, 'she's always lending me religious books, but somehow I don't feel I have much need for God myself.'

We got on so well, we exchanged addresses and I promised to write, but you know how it is. . . . Seven months later, I could not get this girl out of my thoughts one day, so I wrote her a letter just telling her how much God had done for me in the months since we had met. Two days later she replied.

'You will never know how perfectly your letter was timed,' she began. 'I felt that morning that my marriage was over and I could not stay with my husband any longer. I was packing my children's things when the postman came. I had hardly finished reading your letter when my Christian friend popped in. I hadn't seen her for weeks. We had a long talk and a prayer together and I have decided to stick my marriage out, and go with her to church from now on. I felt as if God was getting at me from two directions. Are all of you in league?'

No we are not, but God is in control of His many pairs of gloves!

25: The non-professionals

The marmalade just would not set. I stood stirring it while it heaved and spat at me from the preserving pan. Behind me at the kitchen table sat Zoe, chopping peel and talking like a machine gun. Under the table squatted her little daughter Octavia, content now that she had pulled out the entire contents of every cupboard within her reach and littered every inch of the floor. We let her do it, because if we had tried to stop her she would have done something even more irritating! Zoe had been in her first year at university reading maths, when she found she was pregnant. Now she and Octavia lived a nomadic life, keeping house for men whose wives had left them. As soon as the men 'got fresh' or their children bullied Octavia, they moved on.

'I seem to hit the bottle every evening now,' said Zoe banging the knife down despairingly on the board. 'What am I going to do?'

I pushed the pan off the heat, (the whole batch was burnt anyway.) 'You know,' I said, sitting down at the table beside her, 'I think you ought to get professional help. I'm just not qualified to advise you.'

'I've had enough of social workers and all their kind,' growled Zoe. 'It's just because you are an ordinary mum that I can talk to you.'

Nowadays there are excellent books and courses designed to train people for Christian counselling. Many of my friends, both male and female have decided to become social workers simply because God has opened their eyes to the plight of others.

Sometimes while being used as God's gloves, people discover they have been given a special gift of divine healing or a deep prayer ministry. God may call you further into many specialist fields, but this book was written about ordinary people, doing ordinary things under the control of God. They have probably been caring for people for years instinctively, and never realised what an important job they have been doing!

Danger!

Just because we are so ordinary, we may begin reaching out to other people while still feeling inadequate in many ways, then gradually God builds up our confidence as we see Him working. We learn by our mistakes, so we stop making so many and soon we are deluded into thinking we're pretty good at this job. In fact, we begin to feel like professionals with the answers to everyone's problems instead of the inept amateur that we really are. Not only will we then stop relying on God and so become infinitely less useful, but our superior attitude, will begin to show and the very people we long to help will run for cover.

One evening Tony and I were invited out to supper by Zaida and Dick, whom I mentioned in the chapter 'Caring for the carers'. They had opened their home to four people with very diverse problems, and the other couple they had asked along to meet us were in very much the same 'caring business'. As we sat round the table we began chatting about some of the people who had lived in our various homes. The stories flew backwards and forward, each one funnier than the last, and we positively ached with laughter. There was the incontinent tramp who smelt so bad everyone had to breathe through their mouths and not through their noses. The girl who always managed to fall off her motor scooter as we waved her goodbye at what we hoped was the end of her visit. The ex-junkie whose stomach had been so damaged by heroin that she hiccuped constantly and deafeningly, especially in church. When Dick gave us a demonstration and added to it an impression of an unfortunate young man who had the most appalling stutter, Tony laughed so much he had to lie on the floor, and my face felt positively stiff as we drove home. Then quite suddenly I felt God was not pleased with us. What did we think we were doing looking down on these people from a lofty height and laughing at them in derision?

'How would you cope if you had their backgrounds and problems?' God seemed to say, and all I could think of was the famous quote, 'There but for the grace of God go I'.

Of course, we cannot become too intense and take the burden of their suffering on to our shoulders instead of handing it to God. A sense of humour is vital if we are to keep our own sanity, but we had publicly given the impression that we were professionals talking 'shop' and laughing about our 'amusing cases'.

We are not professionals, only limp, empty gloves. Those people were damaged and broken and God was carefully and painstakingly putting them back together again. He didn't really need our help, but for some strange reason He used it.

Once again, Amy Carmichael sums it all up in her book *If* 'If I belittle those whom I am called to serve, talk of their weak points in contrast perhaps with what I think of as my strong points; if I adopt a superior attitude, forgetting 'who made thee to differ? and what hast thou, that thou hast not received?' Then I know nothing of Calvary love.'

In the year 1500, the young Michelangelo completed an exquisite marble statue – his beloved Pieta. For 472 years it was admired by the world for its perfection. Then one day a demented young man who thought he was Jesus Christ, took a hammer into St. Peter's Basilica in Rome and delivered fourteen terrible blows to this object of complete beauty.

For seven months, the greatest experts in the world laboured in the Vatican laboratories to restore Mary's mutilated face, broken arm and hand. With infinite patience and care, they pieced together the hundreds of chips of marble and at last the statue of Mary holding her dead son looked almost perfect again. Some of the people God needs to love through us will have been damaged by human beings just as brutally as that statue, and in His eyes the junkie with hiccups or the young man who stuttered, are infinitely more precious than this statue that people travel the length of the world to see. Often it takes Him a lifetime of patient work to mend them, and we have to realise that we are often almost as damaged as they are, and He is in the process of mending us as well. Who are we to feel superior or proud? It is not us doing the repair work, but God working through us, damaged and imperfect as we are.

The log in the bog

One morning, not long after the supper party, I was standing at my sink up to my elbows in washing up. I was feeling desperately worried, pressured and unsure of what God really wanted me to do. There were three people I was deeply involved with just then. First there was Cathy, whose husband became violent during a drinking binge causing her, together with her little boy to take refuge in our house, sometimes for several days at a time. Then there was Zoe with her little Octavia who was fast driving me mad, and lastly Diana, whom I mentioned in the chapter 'Love your neighbour'. Her broken leg still had not mended and I was popping in and out of her house frequently. None of the three women knew the Lord yet, and they all required a great deal of my time and energy, while the two small children completely disrupted my house.

'Lord,' I prayed desperately, 'I don't think I can go on coping. Whenever I've felt like this before you've always stepped in. Am I falling into the same old trap of putting other people before my family and my own relationship with You? Please show me what to do.' Knowing God's will is certainly one of the hardest parts of being a Christian, the only thing I've learnt for sure is that He will always stop us from making a mistake if we sincerely ask Him to do so. I fervently hoped He would step in and release me that day, but instead I received one of the most definite pieces of guidance I ever had.

I thought you were supposed to have visions in church, or after days of prayer and fasting, but I had mine standing right there at the kitchen sink, and I don't think I have ever been the same since. I 'saw' a marshy coast line, and the people I was trying to help were clinging together on a hummock of sea grass in a quagmire of sinking mud. Jesus was on the mainland, and they longed to reach Him, but were prevented by the treacherous mud.

'Lord, what can I do to get them across to you? I whispered.

'Lie down on your face in the mud like a log, and let them walk over your back to me.' He replied. 'They will never notice you or remember you, but they will walk to Me in safety. Their feet will hurt your back, and the mud will make you dirty. Are you willing for that?'

As a Christian I paid lip service to the belief that this life is short and unimportant in comparison with eternity, and one soul pulled out of the slime is worth a life time of effort, yet here I was resenting the unloading of my kitchen cupboards, the burning of my marmalade and a mixture of orange squash and chewed biscuit dribbled over my armchairs. It is not very exciting or glamorous being a log in a bog, but the wonderful thing is that all three of those women and their two husbands are now safety on the mainland with the Lord.

What's in it for me?

It would be terrible if I gave the impression that over the last twelve years since the events of the first chapter of this book, life has been a dull, 'muddy', hard working grind. Looking back over the years feels like walking down a long corridor, crammed with fascinating people. Knowing them has changed and enriched our lives and personalities, and they have actually helped us far more than we have helped them. I wondered how our children felt sharing their lives, in view of all the mistakes we have made, so before writing this chapter I asked them.

'It would have been terribly dull just being us,' commented Justyn, and just for once they were all in unanimous agreement!

Rewards but not success

While God certainly promises us many rewards for caring for the needy (Isaiah 58: 7–11, Matt. 6:3 3–4 and Gal. 6:9). He never promises us that our experience of caring will be a 'rose garden' with success at the end of every story. Writing about all the colourful people in that corridor has thrilled me deeply, and proved to me yet again how exciting working for God can be, but it is sad to relate that although in many cases God has rebuilt them, they still have not yet responded to His claim on their lives; we have often felt hurt and rejected. It comforts me to know that the old prophet Samuel felt like that when the people of Israel no longer wanted him. God said in 1 Samuel 8:7 and 8 (GNB), 'You are not the one they have rejected . . . now they are doing to you what they have always done to me.' Do we only feel the pain of failure if we secretly wanted to share the glory of success? Or do we mind because God Himself is being hurt?

Last week the children pushed me into the smartest shop in town to buy a birthday present for Tony. The wheelchair sunk into the rich pile of the carpet and the assistants cooed round us like doves. Suddenly a raucous voice hailed us from the far side of the department, and a very unsteady figure began to lurch towards us. To our horror we saw that it was Will, who has lived with us on and off for the last three ears. He has an alcohol problem that most of the time seems to be cured, but his lapses are dramatic and embarrassing! The assistants ceased to coo, and began to cluck instead. We tried hard to pretend we did not know him, but Will put his arms round my neck and breathed gin into my ear.

'He's drunk!' said the outraged manager when Will began to become obstreperous. Well dressed male assistants hussled him towards the door, while a female hurried behind them spraying an airfreshener.

'Let's get out of here quickly,' we said, our faces red with shame, and I have to admit with anger as well, when I realised the suspicious lightness of my purse had probably made Will's trip to the Off Licence possible!

'Perhaps we'd better go to Woolworths to buy Dad's present,' I said firmly, and we slid out of the shop.

The Lord still loves Will, and we discovered we did too when he turned up next morning, repentant but stinking after having spent the night in the public loo.

Love with your feet as well as with your head!

Earlier that same day, a friend of mine popped in to see me during her lunch hour. She had been ill for two weeks and this was her first day back at work. At first, I thought her drawn white face and uneasy manner were due to the illness, but then I suddenly said, 'Ginny, what's up?'

'I'm worried about something that happened in our house group last night,' she admitted. Ginny comes from a church where they really know how to worship the Lord with spontaneity and joy, and the congregation are also very demonstrative in their love for each other.

'I've been in a lot of really severe pain lately,' explained Ginny, 'and I've been very frightened because the doctor said I'd need major surgery. Actually, the stone that was causing all the trouble passed naturally, but I still feel I've been living through a nightmare, yet no one from church came near me. It was someone who is not even a member who rang me each day, did our bits of shopping and popped in with flowers. When I went to the house group last night, they all said, "We were praying for you so much and thinking of you all the time." I just couldn't help saying, "It would have helped me so much if only I'd known that." They looked so surprised and one person was really offended. I feel terrible now, but it's no good only loving people in your head, the love has to activate your feet and flow through your hands.'

When she had gone back to work, I looked up 1 John 3:11, 16 and 18 (GNB). 'The message you heard from the very beginning is this: we must love one another. . . . This is how we know what love is: Christ gave His life for us. We too, then, ought to give our lives for our brothers! . . . My children, our love should not be just words and talk; it must be pure love, which shows itself in action.' Paul in 1 Corinthians 13 puts love above all other ministries, gifts or fruits of the Spirit, and John says we must love one another because Jesus commanded us to (John 13:34).

'But I do love,' we so easily say, but does that love activate our feet and flow out through our hands in actions?

190

No such thing as a ministry of caring

It is easy to look round our church and see certain people who stand out from everyone else because of their loving concern for others.

'That's their ministry,' we shrug, 'they are called to serve the Lord in that way. Me? I have a ministry of music, so I have to leave the ministry of caring to others.'

I firmly believe there is no such thing as a ministry of caring, given only to certain people, but we all have the responsibility of caring. Of course, we won't all be called to care for people in the same way. I have tried in this book to show the many ways that God uses people with different temperaments, circumstances, material possessions and even problems, to help others. We may be enormously gifted and wealthy, or we may be able to do little more than make soup; we could be an energetic 'Martha', or a bed-ridden invalid; but we all equally have the responsibility to be God's visible representative to the people around us.

The two halves of worship

All down through church history, God has regularly sent great waves of spiritual renewal, and I believe we are seeing the begining of one right now in our life time. As David Pawson says, 'The tide is coming in.'

So why are we surrounded by neighbours, workmates and fellow church-goers who are full of fear, loneliness and despair? Perhaps we fail them because we forget the connection between two little verses in Hebrews 13 (NIV). Verse 15 says, 'Through Jesus, therefore, let us continually offer to God a sacrifice of praise – the fruit of lips that confess His name.' I think in many churches nowadays we are very good at that. We have been released into a marvellous pattern of creative worship, and as we vibrate with all the new music it is easy to praise God with our lips. But verse 16 carries straight on and says, 'And do not forget to do good and to share with others, for with such sacrifices God is pleased.'

To sacrifice and to worship are one and the same thing in the context of this passage. It is easy to feel that when we have been in church on a Sunday, we have been worshipping God, but He recognises that we have also been worshipping Him on a Monday when we buy some flowers for a lonely old lady. We can sacrifice offerings of worship both through our lips and by our acts of kindness. These two verses must stay bound together. One without the other causes an imbalance. We need to hold them tightly, one in either hand.